Explorations in Theo

Explorations in Theology 8

G. W. H. LAMPE

SCM PRESS LTD

334 01979 6

First published 1981
by SCM Press Ltd
58 Bloomsbury Street, London WC1

Photoset by Input Typesetting Ltd
and printed in Great Britain by
Billing & Sons Ltd
London, Guildford and Worcester

Contents

Preface

Geoffrey Lampe learned in August 1980 that he had only a few days to live. He noted down the papers to be included in this volume, indicating alternative versions in some cases, and other material to be added or substituted as seemed appropriate. He set his affairs in order, down to the details of his funeral service, with a Lampean combination of humour, courage and efficiency which, though it characterized all his activity, was in the circumstances astonishing and deeply moving.

In the collection no particular order was specified, except that the piece on preparation for death should come at the end. As arranged here, the first essay, on 'Faith and "The Faith" ', reflects Professor Lampe's lifelong concern for the openness and freedom of Christian faith, openness to the Spirit however it blows, and complete commitment to intellectual, social and political freedom, in the truth of Christ. The essay on 'Salvation' underscores the writer's concern for the central issues in Christian doctrine. A fresh interpretation of the patristic understanding of deification leads to a new appreciation of salvation through Christ today.

The following two pieces offer different perspectives on the Trinity in Christian faith. 'What Future for the Trinity?' is a brilliantly succinct account of the heart of the patristic doctrine, critical of the orthodox position while strongly affirming the divinity of Christ. The Midhurst parish sermon, one of his last, is a profound devotional meditation on the engagement of God the Spirit with human life. The next three essays are mainly exegetical studies for learned *Festschrifts*. 'The Two Swords', an attempt to solve the exegetical riddle of Luke 22.38, is a fascinating example of the process of separating scholarship from pseudo-scholarship. The related papers on Revelation 19.10 and on 'Martyrdom and Inspiration' conclude that the witness to

Jesus through martyrdom is the very essence of prophetic inspiration in the early church, and is part of an underlying and significant 'pneumatology of martyrdom'.

'Women and the Ministry of Priesthood' reflects Geoffrey Lampe's great interest in contemporary church issues, and is a measured but passionate plea for the ordination of women to the priesthood, not as a concession to modernity but as recognition of part of God's purpose for mankind. The essays on 'The "Limuru Principle" and Church Unity' and 'The Essence of Christianity' show a subtle appreciation of tradition as the servant, though not the master, of a creative approach to the future of church and faith. Mere's Commemoration Sermon, on 'Preparation for Death', is a cool and highly perceptive meditation. He had also prepared a bibliography.

Geoffrey Lampe was quite clear that, in an age of much ecclesiastical biography, there should be no 'life' in his case. His theology, he said, was his life. There was of course much more to him than theology. But his faith mattered to him, and made him such a generous and unstinting friend to so many different sorts of people. He was both a liberal and a radical theologian, and there was nothing superficial about either his liberalism or his radicalism. On occasion he would speak out in the name of Christian conscience when more cautious men, playing safe, said nothing. Often he said little but thought and acted instead. He had much sympathy with 'radical modernism' in theology. Yet he had as sharp an eye for truism and fallacy in positions which were in principle congenial to him as in positions with which he disagreed basically. Creator of the *Patristic Greek Lexicon* and of several important books, he was a scholar in a society well-stocked with passable imitations. He represented the best in what was once called a 'liberal evangelical' tradition, a tradition still, as these essays again demonstrate, a source of challenge, illumination and Christian renewal.

In *God as Spirit*, the printed version of his Bampton lectures, Lampe came back again and again to the Spirit of God as the Spirit of Christlikeness as an existential reality in society. In this concentration he came curiously close, though he would not have made the comparison, to that other great theologian of our time, of the Isenheim altarpiece. But his own understanding of the key concept of Christlikeness based on his combination of radical critical thought with classical Christian devotion, was in its most important aspects *sui generis*.

As it has turned out, the production of this collection has been very much a joint effort by Geoffrey and Elizabeth Lampe, and their children Celia and Nicolas.

Cambridge   George Newlands
September 1980

Acknowledgments

We are grateful to editors and publishers for permission to reproduce the essays in this volume from the following:

'Faith and "The Faith" ' from *Living the Faith: A Call to the Church*, ed. Kathleen Jones, Oxford University Press 1980

'Salvation: Traditions and Reappraisals' from *Queens Essays*, ed. J. M. Turner, Birmingham 1980

'What Future for the Trinity?' from *The Cambridge Review*, 17 November 1978

'A Sermon for Trinity Sunday' from *Midhurst Parish Magazine*, July 1980

'The Two Swords' (Luke 22.38)' was written for *Jesus and the Politics of his Day*, ed. E. Bammel and C. F. D. Moule, © Cambridge University Press 1981, and is reproduced here by permission.

' "The Testimony of Jesus is the Spirit of Prophecy" (Revelation 19.10)' from the *Bo Reicke Festschrift*, ed. D. A. Brownell and W. Weinrich, Brill, Leiden, forthcoming

'Martyrdom and Inspiration' from *Suffering and Martyrdom in the New Testament*, ed. W. Horbury, and B. McNeil, Cambridge University Press 1981

'The "Limuru Principle" and Church Unity' from *The Churchman*, Vol. 88 No. 1, 1974

'The Essence of Christianity: A Personal View' from *The Expository Times*, Vol. 87 No. 5, 1976

'Preparation for Death' from *The Epworth Review*, Vol. 7 No. 3, 1980

(In chapters 2, 5, 6 and 7 the biblical references and other short notes have been incorporated into the text, and the remaining notes renumbered.)

Abbreviations

1

Faith and 'The Faith'

Is 'doing theology' a process of discovery, an exploration of human experience in quest of truth about God's dealings with man which we do not yet know? Is the theologian (a term which properly includes every man and woman who tries seriously to think about God) an enquirer who can carry out actual research, asking questions to which satisfying answers have not yet been given, and who, while learning all he can from his predecessors, taking them as his guides, and never rejecting their findings lightly, is nevertheless prepared to discover that in some respects those findings may now be too dated to be useful and in others may turn out to be plainly mistaken? Or, alternatively, is the task of the theologian essentially to rehearse, expound, and where necessary re-state for the sake of greater clarity a body of given truth handed down from the past, from which, since it is ultimately revealed by God himself, it is possible in principle, if the theologian interprets it correctly and intelligibly, to read off all the answers to whatever questions about God and man it is proper and important for us to ask?

The answer which we give to this problem determines our attitude to the nature and role of authority in matters of religious belief, and our ideas about where such authority may be found; our different attitudes to this question are the major cause of the divisions between Christians today. This is the basic issue which cuts across the denominational boundaries, and which also creates much of the impatience, frustration, bewilderment, and defensiveness which affect so many Christians in all the churches.

Behind this problem of authority there stands the question of revelation. To many people this question seems to have become more and more difficult since the breakdown of the old theory which virtually identified the content of revelation with a system of doctrine. It is only a short time in the history of Christian thought since this view of revelation as disclosed in infallibly true propositions broke down and became superseded. It had enjoyed a very long reign. Christians had differed, often violently, on the question of the respective areas of human knowledge and revealed truth, some affirming and others virtually denying the possibility of natural theology: that is, that some truths concerning God could be worked out by men for themselves. They had quarrelled bitterly about where revealed truth could be found: whether in scripture alone, in scripture interpreted by the church's tradition, or in scripture together with the tradition as parallel and independent channels of divine communication. But they were in entire agreement that somewhere, available to all believers, there was a body of teaching imparted by God, consisting of eternal and infallible truths.

The well-worn story of how that agreement came to an end includes the rise of biblical theology: the realization that within the Bible itself revelation does not seem to be understood in those terms; and the insistence of so many theologians in this century that, in William Temple's words, 'What is offered to man's apprehension in any specific revelation is not truth concerning God, but the living God himself.' Gradually theologians came to see that the theological formulations in which the faith of Christian believers has been articulated, and to a considerable extent that basic faith itself, are all conditioned by the culture of their time with its religious, philosophical, and scientific presuppositions, and are not timeless expressions of truths inaccessible to natural human knowledge. They developed fuller appreciation of the diversity of outlook of the biblical writers, so that the New Testament is seen to be the source, not of a single, uniform, doctrinal tradition, but of a plurality of doctrines. Finally, they began to accept the fact that for human beings in this life there is no such thing as an infallible authority, whether Bible, Church, Pope, or any other supposedly inerrant source or guardian of truth, which can guarantee any belief to be true or confer an extrinsic warrant upon any proposition or upon any event that it is to be received as revelatory of God.

Revelation and interpretation

It is in our human experience that revelation is mediated to us. To say that God discloses himself in events may be misleading. This is because there seems to be no event which is such that no one experiencing it, whatever his presuppositions may be, can possibly doubt that in it God is revealed – that it is indeed an act of God. There is always some alternative explanation for it. An atheist might publicly challenge the Almighty to strike him dead. If he should then and there fall down dead, a thorough sceptic could nevertheless call it a coincidence, demand a post-mortem, and either discover some adequate secondary cause of death, or, if none were found, conclude that although the present state of medical knowledge did not enable us to establish why the man died, it was certainly to be expected that the advance of science would one day clear up such apparent mysteries. In the last resort, as the gospels show, an alternative primary cause can always be suggested for what a believer would regard as a revelatory act of God: an event can be acknowledged to be a miracle, but ascribed to the agency of Beelzebub. This means that it is not events in themselves which may be revelatory (and of course we do not have access to bare 'events in themselves'), but events as experienced and interpreted.

The Christian believer conceives of the whole continuous process of creation as the act of God; in the natural order and in the course of history he finds, by faith, a self-revelation of immanent deity. Within this single process he perceives focal points of that self-revelation, and these do, indeed, seem to furnish him with a key to enable him to discern the purposes and activity of God in the entire continuum of history. But the reason why it is only a limited number of special occurrences which provide this key is not that God was active in these to a greater degree than in other happenings. It is, rather, because at these particular points in history there were experiencing human subjects whose interpretations of what took place seem to us, in retrospect, to show that they were people of special insight and discernment, able to perceive that in their experiences there was a self-disclosure of God. Revelation is certainly mediated in events, but not directly. It comes through the inferences which some people draw from them, and it is those inferences which may in certain cases make the event a medium of revelation both to those people themselves and to the rest of us who hear or read about their inferences at second hand. So, then, it is experience as interpreted which may give rise to faith; in and through the thoughts of human beings God discloses himself and evokes that attitude of commitment which we call faith. The Bible is a unique record of human experience of this kind. When we read that 'God spoke to' Abraham or Moses, that 'the word of the Lord came to' a prophet, what we are being told in the first instance is that Abraham and Moses *thought* that God was speaking to them; the prophet *believed* that he had received a message from the Lord.

I am not implying by this that the experience of the believer is nothing more than an experience of his own imaginings. On the contrary, the believer's conviction that he has been truly and actually addressed by God is open to rational examination, to testing in the light of his own experience as a whole and of the experience of other people present and past, to the test of practical experiment (living out the conviction that this interpretation is true), and to the criterion, 'by their fruits you shall know them'. It need not be an irrational belief. Its truth can never be proved, for it is a matter of faith, but it can be commended and imparted to others, and recognized as a true insight into the stuff of reality, an apprehension of the way things are – that is to say, accepted as revelation. We possess a canon of scripture essentially because the interpreted experience recorded in those books has broadly commended itself to all subsequent generations as revelatory; that the insight which drew such inferences from experienced events was sound and true. That brings us close to the concept of inspiration.

It is often said that in the Bible the word of God is communicated in the words of men. But it seems that, not only in the Bible but always, the word of God is mediated in human thoughts. Both sides of this relationship should be emphasized: the word of *God*; the thoughts and imagination and emotions of *human* people. This means that, although there is certainly a great difference between 'faith' (which we are considering now) and 'the Faith' as a structured body of beliefs, between experience interpreted as revelatory on the one hand, and theological analyses and articulations of that revelatory experience on the other, yet we must be careful how we try to express this difference. It would be an over-simplification to say that 'faith' refers to immediate awareness of God, and that 'the Faith' is the result of subsequent theological reflection upon this awareness, gradually elaborated into an organized system of beliefs. The truth appears rather to be that the primary data of faith which form the raw material, as it were, for theology, are themselves inferences from experienced events, and that the difference between 'faith' and 'the Faith' is not, therefore, simply a difference between direct awareness and inference, but a difference between a first stage of inference and a second stage of inference.

I am not particularly concerned here with the well-worn distinction between 'belief in' and 'belief that'. It is true that a believer's response to God's self-disclosure will be hope and trust ('belief in'). It is equally true that there cannot be a response of personal faith which does not involve 'belief that'. What I am concerned with is this theory that faith is not a mode of direct experience, or, to put it another way, a mode of primary apprehension, but an inference from, or interpretation of, experience.

In attempting to distinguish the primary data of faith, that is to say revelation, from the secondary interpretations which theology places upon those data and which form the groundwork of doctrinal systems, some theologians have suggested that the primary data, the content of revelation, are a direct awareness of God. If this were so, then the task of theological reconstruction could begin on a solid foundation; for if faith were an immediate consciousness of God, it would afford us as firm a given reality as our consciousness of other people. Faith could then claim to be a mode of knowledge. That being so, the task of the theologian would simply be to state and explain the content of this knowledge in the most adequate terms available. In fact, however, this does not seem to be the case. Professor Leonard Hodgson once wrote:

> The words 'I believe' in the Creed mean both less and more than 'I know'. 'I believe' means *less* than 'I know'. This is important in the interests of intellectual honesty. Religious creeds are concerned with the most profound, indeed the ultimate, mysteries, with problems concerning which only a fool or a knave could claim to have knowledge. . . . It is by implying a resolve to live by what is affirmed that 'I believe' means *more* than 'I know'.[1]

This may be a rather unfashionable account of faith nowadays,

but I think it is true as against the claim that faith is an immediate awareness of God. Even in the case of the saint who
has the strongest conviction that he is actually being addressed
by God it is still appropriate to speak of the 'venture' of faith.
For faith is an interpretation put upon events, and as such it is
necessarily tentative and hypothetical. To embrace the interpretation which Christian faith puts upon our experience is in some
respects parallel to the adoption of a scientific hypothesis. It
has to be tried in practice to find out whether it holds good.

Better, perhaps, is an analogy with some other kinds of insight and perception. A good comparison has been drawn between the perspective of faith in which we may interpret our
experience and the 'arrangement' or composition of a picture,
a piece of music, or a roomful of furniture which seems to us,
once we have hit upon it, to be exactly 'right'. This sense of
rightness seems to be intuitive; but we can analyse it and give
reasons to ourselves for feeling it so certainly, we can invite
other people to see it our way and we can, at any rate to a
certain extent, show them rationally why we think they should
see it like that. Some people would perhaps say here that the
insight of faith involves a much more profound reorientation of
one's entire personality than this analogy suggests. It is not just
a question of hitting on a satisfying angle from which to view
one's life; it is not like arranging the furniture; it is more like
falling in love and *finding* one's life transformed rather than
deliberately remodelling it. That is certainly true; but two points
need to be considered here.

First, the rightness of the satisfying composition, or even of
the transformation brought about by falling in love, is different
from the provable correctness of the answer to a mathematical
problem. Secondly, it is nevertheless entirely possible to find
and to state rational grounds on which to defend and to
advocate the adoption of this perspective. The idea that faith is
itself a gift of God is true; but this certainly does not mean that
it is infused into the believer by a miracle, an act of God which
bypasses his human reason, will, and feelings.

The analogy of falling in love does, however, bring out the
fact that faith is commitment and an attitude of response. It
may begin, whether at the level of our relationship with other
people or of our response to God, with an almost unformed
sense of being confronted by something or someone wonderful:
a compulsion to respond such as we read about in the gospels

when Jesus said to men who had apparently never met him before, 'Follow me', and they got up and followed him. Of course, a rudimentary faith of this kind is accompanied almost at once by a desire to discover and articulate rational grounds for it; reasons, for instance, for one's extraordinary confidence in this particular person. If we do not want so much to reason it out for our own sake, we have to try to do so as soon as there is any question of communicating our feelings to other people, and most of all when we need to defend them against opponents. So commitment involves beliefs, almost from the first, and beliefs are the groundwork of the articulated structure of 'the Faith'.

The believer, however, always experiences faith as response to a divine initiative, to God's approach to, and encounter with, himself. This is the interpretation which he puts on events, the perspective in which he sees them. For the nature of that initiative and encounter he finds the language of claim, demand, grace, calling, appropriate. In fact the classic accounts of faith responding to revelation, those which have always seemed to be paradigmatic for the experience of successive generations, suggest that the response is not so much to any disclosure of abstract truth, certainly not so much to any knowledge or revelation of theological truths, as to a call to action, to the discharge of some concrete task. Paul's vision on the Damascus road, as Luke describes it, was not in the first instance a disclosure of truth about Christ, though much christology could be, and was, inferred from it, but a call to bring the Gentiles into the kingdom of God. Some form of vocation to an actual missionary task seems to be central in most of the stories of the Easter appearances. One could continue to quote examples, for revelation seems characteristically to be mediated in a person's overwhelming conviction that he is called to undertake a specific task, and faith to be a response carried out in action rather than a conversion to a particular theology.

The practice of faith

It is certainly in action that faith is tested. It is, admittedly, extremely difficult to establish any criteria by which the interpretation which faith places upon experience can be verified or falsified. It may be measured against other inferences which may be drawn from experience, such as those which the facts

of suffering and evil may suggest, but even that kind of comparison and weighing can scarcely be carried out effectively in
the abstract, for instance in academic essays. The only real
means of testing faith is to live by it. This is why Professor
Hodgson spoke of faith being more than knowledge, because
it implies a resolve to live by what is affirmed. This testing,
however, seems to be of a rather peculiar kind. Preachers often
invite their hearers to make the venture of faith, to gamble
everything, as it were, on the truth of this interpretation of our
human experience, to try it out and see if it works. It is not
usually suggested as a serious possibility that they might find
that it doesn't work. And this is not because the preacher is
unrealistic or afraid to face an unpleasant possibility. It is rather
because it is so hard to see what would make a person conclude
that in fact faith doesn't work. For one cannot really start this
experiment in a neutral or agnostic frame of mind; you cannot
act as if you were making a faith response to revelation without
actually committing yourself, since faith is commitment. And if
you are once committed it is difficult indeed to conceive of any
situation in which your experience will persuade you that your
commitment is misguided, your perspective on life is, after all,
not the 'right' one. One can easily envisage circumstances in
which it might *seem* that the Christian interpretation of life had
proved false; the prayers that appear to have gone unanswered,
the failure of a person or a cause that one certainly believed to
be in accordance with God's will, and therefore trusted would
succeed; the failure of Christianity to meet a decisive challenge,
like that which is presented to it now by the relations between
the white and black races or the economic disparity between
the rich and poor nations, and perhaps the possibility of a
non-Christian religion or system of belief succeeding where
Christians fail. But a faith which is centred upon the cross will
not easily be dismayed by the apparently unanswered prayer,
or the apparent defeat of God's purposes, or the destruction of
his servants; and one who has made the venture of faith and
committed himself to trying it out is likely to reject the suggestion that in a case like that of race relations Christian faith has
been shown not to work. He will probably say, on the contrary,
that it has not been fully tried; what is needed is not an alternative to Christianity but much more of it. This is not to pretend
that no one can try out a Christian perspective on life and come
to the negative conclusion that it doesn't work. Some very fully

committed believers have experienced what amounts to a conversion, closely parallel to conversion to faith, in the opposite direction: from a specifically Christian attitude to non-theistic humanism. For them it has not worked. At the same time, however, it often happens that although they abandon their Christian or theistic standpoint, their commitment to certain values, such as justice, brotherhood and compassion, which they had previously articulated in theistic terms, remains; that basic commitment still works. It is difficult to imagine a person so committed deliberately, and after full and careful reflection, embracing an attitude of aggressive selfishness as a matter of principle.

The test of practice, the criterion, 'By their fruits you shall know them', has to be applied, too, to rival and incompatible claims to have experienced revelation. Not all interpretations of experience as revelatory can be true. It is important that this should be stressed. A Christian cannot rest content with a purely sociological evaluation of faiths, which takes no account of the question of the truth of their content. Indeed, he must go further and claim that the relationship of God to man and of man to God realized concretely in the life of Jesus, the relationship of fatherhood and sonship in which trusting obedience answers to divine love and, in turn, becomes the channel of divine love to other human beings, is the pattern and norm for him for all interpretations of experience as revelatory of God. Whatever actually contradicts that pattern must be rejected. At the same time, once again, at the deep level of commitment which lies beneath all the differences in articulated systems of belief and formulated theologies, the area of agreement among people of different faiths concerning the values by which they intend to live, and for which sometimes they would be prepared to die, is very broad and comprehensive.

Yet the practice of faith, the process of living by what one affirms, may well result in a modification of its content, even though the general overall commitment remains. This may happen in the case of an individual believer, and more strikingly in the case of a believing community. It is not only systems of theology, 'the Faith', which undergo changes in the course of time. Faith itself, the response to experience interpreted as divine-human encounter, may itself change, so that God's dealings with us come to be differently understood. An example of this is the impossibility nowadays of using the occasional

prayers and the service for the visitation of the sick provided in
the Book of Common Prayer; for these presuppose the belief
that pestilence, famine and illness are deliberately sent by God
as punishments to induce sinners to repent or as tests of faith
and patience for the righteous. Most of us do not share that
belief. It survives today chiefly in a vestigial form in the familiar
question asked by unfortunate sufferers and their friends, 'What
have I done (or 'what has he or she done') to deserve this?'
Fortunately it is usually a rhetorical question. They don't really
expect the answer, 'Well, I'll tell you what you've done. You
bullied your little sister when you were a child, and when you
grew up you fiddled your tax, and so God has very properly
handed you down a coronary.' Here is a real change in the basic
faith-interpretation of life. In this sort of way practice, continuing experience, tests what we *really* believe.

Does this mean, then, that revelation can change? It certainly
means that our apprehension and understanding of revelation
can and does change. For revelation comes to us in and through
the inferences we draw from experience. It does not come as
direct awareness of God; we can never have revelation 'neat' as
it were, and we do not have access to absolute unchanging
truth. It is always communicated in our human thoughts and
feelings which are limited, fallible, and sinful. What was once
seen as revelatory, whether in the Bible or elsewhere, may cease
to communicate revelation; though it is always possible that in
changing historical circumstances, or in the changing circumstances and outlook of an individual, it may become revelatory
once again.

Nevertheless, at any given time, the authority for us of a faith
which we are prepared to live by is supreme. It may, in fact,
possess a life and death authority, for faith is the motive and
inspiration of martyrdom.

This kind of authority does not seem to belong to that second
stage of inference which results in the formulation of beliefs
and their organization into theological structures. The doctrines
of the Faith are not, as used to be supposed, identical with
revelation. Yet although the data of faith are distinguishable
from the forms of thought in which we find them expressed
and explicated, we cannot easily separate the basic insights
which give rise to faith from the philosophical structures in
which they have been built up and articulated as theologies.
When these structures appear to need refurbishing or replacing

we cannot simply break them open, as if we were cracking a nut, extract a solid core of basic faith and transfer it into a repaired and improved, or perhaps brand new, shell of articulated theology. Faith in the end determines and controls the shape of the dogmatic systems of belief which are intended to provide a rational account of it; but these systems themselves react upon and condition the faith which they seek to express. Theological presuppositions themselves give rise to faith. Moses, for example, would not have interpreted his experience at the burning bush in the way he did, had he not already been a believer in the God of Abraham, Isaac, and Jacob. Bernadette's vision came to her in terms of the highly sophisticated theological concept of the Immaculate Conception, itself a product of reflection upon a particular, and again highly complex and difficult, understanding of original sin. Here it seems to be 'the Faith' which gives rise to faith, rather than, as we usually suppose to be the case, faith which acts as the data or raw material for the intellectual process which builds up 'the Faith'. So, then, in trying to distinguish the basic core of faith as a primary inference from experience from the structure of secondary theological inference in which it has become encapsulated, we have to be careful that we are not embarking on the task of peeling an onion.

The use of doctrine

It is, however, broadly true that the task of theology is to reflect upon, articulate, and provide a rational account of the experience in which men have found revelation and of the faith by which they have responded to it. Such of the conclusions of theology as commend themselves to believers generally and are at any given time accepted as the best and truest account of the data with which they are concerned, take on the status of doctrine, and together form the system which we call 'the Faith'. Yet at best they can only be tentative and provisional. Some stand the test of time and of continuing critical examination so well that they seem unlikely to need substantial modification. Some, indeed, seem to be absolutely necessary from the very start of the process of inference, if any sense at all is to be made of the primary revelatory experience, for example, the interpretation of experience in terms of God and God's activity towards human beings. The stage of theological interpretation which consists in theism seems to be entirely inseparable from basic faith. It remains true, however, generally speaking, that doctrines serve the believer in a somewhat similar way to that in which scientific models serve the natural scientist, not for the purpose of making prediction possible, but for analysis of the data of faith. Their authority resides in their usefulness for that purpose, and it is part of the task of theology to criticize its own models and to reflect critically on the faith which these models articulate and express. When changes occur in that faith, or when the doctrinal systems cease to represent the insights of faith adequately – in other words, when they cease to give an acceptable rationale of what we *really* believe – then they have to be revised and modified or even replaced. This applies to all doctrines. The first task in this process is to enquire what actual belief is being expressed; another very important task is to ensure that any modifications in traditional formulations, and any replacements for such formulations, offer as full an account as the original doctrines of that which is in fact believed; and these tasks are by no means easy.

These tasks, however, demand from us certain attitudes. One is that we must not confuse faith with 'the Faith'. This would be rather like identifying 'faith' in James's sense of 'assent' to such a theological proposition as that God is one, with Paul's faith in the sense of total response to justifying grace. We must not, on the other hand, suppose that we can simply dispense with theological structures. Hebrew religion, it is true, articulated its faith insights in terms of worship and conduct rather than of creeds and dogma. But the differentiating factor in Christianity is the place which it gives to Jesus Christ, and this demands christological reflection which in turn requires the formulation of particular beliefs about God. We cannot escape the need for an elaborated theology. But we must not imagine that assent to theological propositions is identical with the commitment of faith and therefore important for salvation. The great error seems to be the idea that because a particular formulation is recognized at some stage in Christian history as constituting 'the Catholick Faith' it therefore follows that 'except a man believe' it faithfully 'he cannot be saved'. We should recognize that the Catholic creeds possess a special degree of authority as theological formulations for the very reason that they are catholic: they have commended themselves to believers generally as acceptable formulations of the implications of their faith. Yet we must not ignore the fact that even those Christians who accept the ancient creeds most whole-heartedly cannot really mean precisely the same things when they repeat them as did those who first framed them. The presuppositions with which, and the intellectual context within which, we now say the words of the Nicene fathers are so different from those of the fourth century that the words themselves cannot convey precisely the same sense to us, however hard we may try to recreate their original significance. In the last resort we must acknowledge that the creeds, like all other articles and confessions, are tentative and provisional human attempts to express and clarify the inferences which faith draws from experience. They are not direct embodiments of revealed truth.

This should mean that in place of the old distinction between the 'teaching church' and the 'learning church', the whole church must be regarded as a body engaged in a co-operative task of learning. In so far as the church has a teaching ministry, this is a form of adult education, conducted by mutual questioning, discussion, and instruction, rather than a kind of infant teaching in which information is handed down authoritatively. Where theology is a corporate enterprise of believers engaged in an open search for truth concerning their experience, Whitehead's dictum ceases to be true, that wherever there are creeds there is a heretic round the corner, or in his grave. There is still a clear distinction between belief and unbelief, but the possibility of drawing clear lines of demarcation between orthodoxy and heresy disappears. Instead, there may perhaps appear the possibility of a new unity, arrived at not through the affirmation of agreed answers but through co-operation in asking questions, and the possibility, too, that such an enterprise may be informed by the spirit of William Temple's memorable dictum: 'To admit acrimony in theological discussion is in itself more fundamentally heretical than any erroneous opinions upheld or condemned in the course of the discussion.'

2

Salvation: Traditions and Reappraisals

I was a student at Queen's, Birmingham, during the academic year 1936–37, preparing for ordination. At that time our Principal, Canon J. O. Cobham, recently translated from the Vice-Principalship of Westcott House and from a Cambridge theological scene increasingly dominated by Hoskyns and his followers, was introducing us to Barthian neo-orthodoxy in an Anglican doctrinal framework and a 'Prayer Book Catholic' liturgical setting. In the close contacts which were established under 'Jock's' leadership with German theologians, and especially in the exchange of visits with the staff and students of the Evangelical *Stift* at Tübingen, we found ourselves exposed in sermons and lectures to a somewhat more dogmatically uncompromising presentation of the theology of 'the Word of God'. With the problem of revelation apparently thus solved, although in fact it had only been temporarily by-passed by a road which has since turned out to lead to a dead end, a solid basis seemed to have been secured for a unified and systematic biblical theology. The radical questioning of traditional christology and trinitarian doctrine by liberal Anglicans such as Rashdall, Major and Bethune-Baker, and the fierce controversy on these basic issues which followed the famous Girton Conference of 1921, had apparently died away. The questions raised by the Liberal Protestantism of the earlier years of the century seemed in the light of neo-orthodox certainties to have been the wrong questions to ask. The main issues and the principal causes of division within the Church of England were those concerning the nature of the church, the ministry and the sacraments, as they continued to be for many years after my time at Queen's. Reports of inter-church conversations during the 1950s and

1960s were usually able to lay stress on the unity which the participants already shared in the greater and more fundamental part of the Christian system of belief: no divisions existed between them in respect of the authority of the biblical revelation, and of the doctrines of God, the person of Christ, the Holy Spirit and Christ's redemptive work. The difficult problems lay in the area of the church and the sacraments, particularly in the controversial questions concerning church order.[1] Even the report, *Doctrine in the Church of England*, the work of a commission appointed in 1922 amidst the repercussions of the Girton Conference, was able to claim in 1938 that the doctrines of God and the Trinity were not matters of controversy.[2] Hence it devoted 16 of its 242 pages to these subjects, as against 102 to the church, the ministry and the sacraments.

After forty years and more, the position is dramatically different. The problems of church order have not, indeed, been solved. They are still fully capable of keeping the churches apart at the institutional level. A different approach to them, however, has gradually rendered them less acute, and far less divisive in actual practice at the level of local congregations. This approach is, broadly speaking, empirical and realistic, aiming at the formulation of doctrine on the basis of, and in the light of, common interdenominational experience of shared life and worship, rather than at compelling the concrete realities of that experience to confine themselves within forms deduced from *a priori* dogma. The existence of an ecumenical Queen's College testifies to the possibilities to which such an approach can lead. The great divisive issues, on the other hand, are seen now to lie in the area of those fundamental doctrines of the classical creeds which the inter-church negotiators of thirty and forty years ago confidently assumed to be matters of general agreement. It is the unfinished business of nineteenth- and early twentieth-century Christian thought, put aside for a time during the period of 'biblical theology', which now claims prior attention, and it is in the field of problems concerning the sources and norms of belief, criteria of truth-claims in Christianity and in religions generally, the relation of articulated systems of belief ('the Faith') to 'faith' by which people actually live, the understanding and interpretation of the person and work of Christ, and the effect of christology upon the doctrine of God, that controversy is now, and is likely to continue to be, most acute. It is not now inter-church controversy; it divides the member-

ship of every Christian communion that takes theology seriously, and it cuts across all the denominational boundaries.

It would seem to be the christological aspects of the current
controversies which most concern the general Christian public.
The question of the meaning of 'salvation', 'redemption', 'atonement', and the other concepts in which traditional theology has
sought to articulate the Christian understanding of the work of
Christ, has not been extensively raised as a pressing issue in
itself. It has, however, often been pointed out that from the
time of the New Testament writers to the present day it is
deeply-rooted convictions about salvation which have determined the pattern of christology, and so, also, the form in
which the doctrine of God and trinitarian theology has been
expressed. This is true of the decisively important period of the
early councils and the classical creeds. The Nicene faith rested
ultimately on the soteriological convictions that it is through
Christ that we are saved, and that what we understand by
'being saved' could not be effected by one who was less than
God in the fullest possible sense of 'God'. It was based on the
application to soteriology of the principle, everywhere accepted
as axiomatic although it scarcely seems to be self-evident, that
what is received by participation, or as a gift, and is not possessed by nature as an inherent property, cannot be passed on
to others. It is sufficient for the recipient alone. For this reason,
according to Athanasius and the Cappodocian fathers, none but
a Christ who is consubstantial with the Father can save, nor can
either an Arian Logos or a Macedonian Holy Spirit, alien in
essence from the Father and deified only by participation in
God through grace, give life or sanctify.

Yet, just because it grew out of, and was determined by,
beliefs about salvation, the Nicene faith in fact made the christological problem insoluble. The Christ of Athanasius and Cyril
of Alexandria is our saviour because he is the consubstantial
Logos who, being unchangeable (*atreptos*), is able to save because he cannot succumb to sin. His divine power overcomes
the weakness and sin of humanity and, while himself remaining
unchanged, he unites manhood to deity and raises it as an
offering to the Father.[3] Cyril's theology made it possible to
assert that the Incarnation was an incarnation of the consubstantial Logos postulated by the faith of Nicaea. It did so, however, only at the necessary cost of denying the full reality of the
Incarnation itself; Cyril's Logos conquers temptation, not in a

genuinely human struggle, smiting 'in man for man the foe', but automatically. On the other side of the great fifth-century controversy, the Antiochenes implicitly denied the full reality of the Incarnation for the opposite reason: in order to safeguard the full reality of the saviour's humanity. By his participation in our actual humanity Christ effects its salvation. To assert this, however, the Antiochene theologians had to pay the necessary price of denying a real incarnation of the consubstantial Logos postulated by the Nicene faith; they had to separate the Logos from the 'assumed man'. In these ancient controversies which produced the theology of Nicaea and the Chalcedonian definition of christology, beliefs and presuppositions concerning salvation determined the pattern of classical christology. Those soteriological convictions, however, proved unable to avoid running into a christological impasse so long as they rested on two assumptions which were treated as axiomatic: the impassibility of God, and the hypostatic existence of the Nicene Logos as the consubstantial Son of God.

Since christology in the past has always been determined in the last resort by the beliefs of Christians concerning their salvation, it is reasonable to suppose that the radical reappraisals of traditional christology which are now being undertaken must involve a thorough re-examination of soteriology: an exploration of how Christians at the present time actually experience the 'saving work of Christ' and what theological models may best serve to articulate this. It is not the intention of this essay to embark on such a task, still less to attempt to suggest how the diverse understandings of salvation which would be disclosed by such an investigation could be related to various types of christology. I only wish to call attention to certain aspects of traditional soteriology which might prove helpful in the reappraisal of beliefs about salvation, and consequently about christology, which would naturally follow such an enquiry.

It is never an easy task to discover what people actually believe about salvation through Christ. It is no less difficult to derive any coherent presentation of soteriology from most of the writings of theologians, apart from those who have tried specifically to formulate some specific account of it. The reason for this lack of clarity is, paradoxically, the very fact that the affirmation that through the work of God in Christ men have been, or are being, or will be, saved lies at the heart of the Christian gospel and has always been central in the tradition of preaching, teaching and liturgy. This means that it is commonly expressed in the conventional language of piety, in phrases that are familiar both to the preacher or writer and to his congregation or readers; their meaning is taken for granted and not analysed or explained. This is already the case even in the earliest post-New Testament writings. In the Apostolic Fathers the idea of salvation is already being expressed in terms which even then had had a long history within the New Testament period in the tradition of popular piety. Preaching, teaching, letter-writing and liturgy are full of biblical echoes, using conventional imagery of light and darkness, truth and error, life and death, knowledge and ignorance. These are sometimes combined, though only rarely in the Apostolic Fathers themselves, with the idea of cleansing from sin and of deliverance through the sacrifice of Christ and the outpouring of his blood.[4]

Neither the writers and preachers nor their audiences are any more likely to have stopped to analyse the precise meaning of this familiar imagery than preachers and their congregations today. In the new Anglican rite of baptism the sponsors are asked, 'Do you turn to Christ?' It is assumed that what this means is perfectly clear, but the imagery, compounded of the ancient pictures of conversion as a turning from darkness to light (Acts 26.18), error to truth, the power of the devil to God, pagan idolatry to the service of the one true God (I Thess. 1.9), and of repentance as a 'turning' (in the language of the Hebrew scriptures), is scarcely likely to awaken an immediate response in the minds of present-day christening parties, without, at any rate, a good deal of imaginative explanation. So, too, generations of children might have sung the words of the old hymn,

> He died that we might be forgiven
> He died to make us good,
> That we might go at last to heaven,
> Saved by his precious blood.

The language has become so familiar that very few people among those who know it by heart have paused to ask what precisely those lines mean, even though to a theologian's eye almost every word in them seems to be crammed full of the most profound problems. Most church-goers, no doubt, are ready to affirm that they have indeed been saved, or will be saved, by Christ's precious blood, although they might find it hard to say from what they have been, or will be, saved, and for what, or to what end, they have been, or will be saved – harder still to say how it is that the blood of Christ has effected, or will effect, this salvation.

Traditional answers which have been given to these questions would, of course, include the belief that by the once-for-all historical event of Christ's death and resurrection we have been saved from the devil in whose power we were held captive as members of a fallen race. Associated with this model of salvation are the evocative images of redemption (a metaphor either of the prisoner-of-war camp whose guards have been overcome and whose gates have been opened by a stronger power, or of the purchase of a slave from a tyrannical master by a benevolent third party with the intention of emancipating him), the Exodus from Pharaoh's country and the entry into the promised land through the baptismal waters, the death of Christ as a sacrifice to avert the power of evil, or as a deception of the devil who is induced to seize the incarnate Son of God in exchange for his rightful victims and then finds that he cannot hold him. Elements in this mythical picture may still find a place in the language of liturgy (they are prominent in some popular Easter hymns), but it cannot correspond to what most people actually believe salvation to mean.

Another answer would find expression in terms of a once-for-all act of deliverance from the wrath of God and condemnation at the final judgment. With this interpretation there is linked the idea of Christ's death as a propitiatory sacrifice or as a vicarious penalty, and an understanding of the human condition as one in which all mankind, as a fallen race, is guilty in the sight of God. Obvious difficulties in the way of maintaining this model of salvation include not only the ethical objections to ideas of vicarious punishment but the prior and major offence caused to many Christians by the casting of God in the role of an infinitely savage hanging judge – an offence which is only increased by the notion that God avoids the dilemma, posed by Athanasius, of either allowing his creatures, made in his image, to be destroyed or of retracting the sentence already decreed against them, by undergoing their death himself in the person of the incarnate Logos.

On the other hand, to interpret salvation as deliverance from sin itself, rather than from God as the judge of sinners, is still meaningful, sin being understood as alienation from God through the choice of self-centredness (expressed in selfishness and exploitation) as a principle of life, in preference to the God-centredness (expressing itself in faith and hope in God and love towards one's neighbour) for which we are created and in which our true being is realized. The forms in which this concept of salvation commends itself are likely to be somewhat different from those of the past. It has been affected by the recognition that the 'story' of the Fall is a myth of our present selfish repudiation of the Creator's love and care, and not a history of an actual event in the process of human evolution. Nor is there generally that intense, individual, 'conviction of sin', in the sense of personal guilt and direct responsibility, which was evoked by such evangelism as that of Wesley. No doubt this is partly due to the post-Freudian and post-Marxian recognition of the severely limited character of individual personal freedom of action and responsibility, probably, also to the gradual, steady, but quite largely tacit, rejection by Christian people of Augustine's disastrous notion that sexual desire and activity is a primary expression of irrational and ungodly selfishness (*concupiscentia*). For if sex is equated with sin, then sin is indeed universal, inescapable, and irresistible and none are free from personal guilt. It seems probable that sin is more generally seen today in terms of social evil (of which racialism would be one instance) rather than primarily of individual disobedience towards God, though of course the one must involve the other. Salvation, then, must have a social and corporate reference; its scope must embrace the redemption of man in society with all the complexity of his personal relationships to others.

With this idea of salvation from sin there are connected the traditional images of expiation (Christ's work being interpreted as the 'putting away' or 'removal' of sin) and the reconciliation of man to God. The Pauline concept of reconciliation (II Cor. 5.18–20), as has often been observed, makes a particularly strong appeal to present-day believers, for it points to the ending of individual estrangement from God and, beyond this, to the renewal, through communion with God, of human society collectively, the ending of conflict between man and man, and of rescue from human exploitation and oppression of the world of man's environment which Paul pictured as waiting with eager longing (Rom. 8.19) for human beings to realize their true nature as children of God.

When salvation is understood on these lines, the death of

Christ may still be seen to have a central and focal place, not, however, as a conquest of the devil (except as a metaphorical expression for the conversion of human sinners), nor as a propitiation of divine wrath or a vicarious execution of a divine death-sentence, but rather as the climax, culmination, and fulfilment of his entire life of faith, love and obedience and as the point where the essential character of 'sonship' towards God is most fully disclosed. Salvation, however, is not then something which was completed once for all in that single past event. It is rather a continuing process towards an eschatological consummation, a process by which the Spirit of God transforms us into the likeness of Christ, the image of God in which we are created, through a 'daily dying' to self-centredness and a continuing 'resurrection' to new life centred in God. The historical Jesus' life of sonship, with the cross as its seal, furnishes the ground and the motive power of the whole process, but that life becomes contemporary, corporate, and potentially universal, as it comes to be re-presented in the community of his followers. The negative sense of salvation as 'being saved from' thus passes over into the positive sense according to which 'being saved' is equivalent to being 'made whole'. Salvation can then be seen as continuous with, and as the completion of, the creation of man.

The promise of 'wholeness' seems to correspond at many levels to the most acutely felt needs of our time. We patently need to be rescued from inadequacy and incompleteness, from the ignorance and blindness which, perhaps more than deliberate evil intention, lie at the root of the human predicament, from our constant failure as individuals to accept ourselves (and so also to accept our fellow beings) and from the guilt and distortions of personal relations which ensue from this, from the perversion of even the best human endeavours by selfishness and greed, and from our collective inability, therefore, to subordinate the advantage of the individual to the common good, to achieve such equality as is possible, to live at peace, and to use the world and its resources properly as stewards of its Creator. Salvation in the sense of personal and social 'wholeness' is synonymous with the coming of the kingdom of God.

To develop an understanding of salvation along these lines does not seem to demand a new soteriology, but rather a reappraisal and reshaping of many elements in the extraordinarily rich tradition of classical thought. Even though patristic theo-

logy ran into grave christological difficulties as a result of some
of its soteriological presuppositions, there are certain elements
in the thought of the early fathers about salvation which seem
especially worth such a reappraisal.

There is no uniformity in their thought about salvation: yet
certain basic areas of agreement are present beneath the diverse
forms of expression used by authors who stand so far apart as
even Tertullian and Origen. They agree that, in its broadest
terms, salvation means positively a process by which man
comes to be in communion with God, and negatively a process
by which he is freed from alienation from God and purified or
redeemed (to use different images) from whatever it is that cuts
him off from God, the source of life. The reason for the wide
variety of forms in which this basic pattern appears is primarily
that these writers start from different presuppositions about
man's condition, and therefore naturally have different ideas
about the way in which it needs to be remedied. All agree that
salvation means deliverance from mortality; but some, in expressing this, lay great emphasis on salvation from actual physical death (the general modern acceptance of bodily death as
natural and not a consequence of a moral 'Fall' makes this
aspect of traditional theology seem strange to us), while others,
like Ignatius,[5] identify 'incorruptibility' with spiritual life, the
Johannine 'eternal life'. For Origen, indeed, the latter is the
only possible interpretation of incorruptibility, since he believes
that the soul was created as pure spirit and that salvation means
its return to its original state. Resurrection therefore means for
him the replacement of the flesh by a purely spiritual body.
Other thinkers, however, who believe that man was created as
a mixture of the spiritual and the physical, hope for the salvation
of the whole man, including, in some sense, his physical nature.

Certain differences of emphasis, again, are due to the extent
to which patristic writers inclined to one side or the other of
the knife-edge that they had to tread in working out their beliefs
about the nature of the soul. On the one hand, it belongs to the
spiritual world and its kinship is with the angels and God; on
the other, it is created and belongs with the material world to
the realm of creatures, which includes everything that is not
God. The tension between these two views is especially marked
in Gregory of Nyssa, within whose works different approaches
to this problem are to be discerned, with correspondingly different attitudes towards the resurrection of the body; for, as the

Gnostics realized, if the soul belongs by nature to the world of pure spirit and is a portion of the divine, the resurrection of the body is irrelevant to its salvation. If, however, as Gregory usually maintains, man is essentially composite, salvation is not salvation unless it includes man's physical nature, however transformed, within its scope.

Much, too, depends upon presuppositions about the relation of the world to God. If it is thought that the prince of this world is the devil and that the whole world lies in the power of the evil one, then salvation means being saved out of the world and from the hostile power that controls it. This aspect of salvation is characteristic of the literature of martyrdom, and there are echoes of it among the early ascetics and hermits. Here, again, there is tension, this time between soteriology and the doctrine of creation. Not only Gnostics and Marcionites, but also some orthodox thinkers, found it easy to think of salvation as an act by which God liberates men from the tyranny of the prince of this world and brings them into a quite new relationship with himself, as sons by adoption. How is this to be related to the doctrine of creation and the belief that, by virtue of being God's creatures, 'in him we live and move and have our being'? A similar problem arises in respect of some contemporary theologies for which the traditional model of incarnation seems essential in order to support an interventionist idea of salvation – the work of Christ being seen as a divine breakthrough into an alien world.

Another source of tension can be discerned in Irenaeus' understanding of salvation as 'recapitulation'. As God's creature, man possesses the divine image. In one aspect this resides in his flesh, so that the image is that of the incarnate Son. It also consists in the freedom of man's rational will, in his mastery over his own acts and over the rest of creation. Adam also had the potentiality of progress in the likeness of God, which is the possession of the Spirit which should have enabled him to advance to perfection. Since, however, Adam was defeated by the devil and lost the 'likeness', and since all men were included in Adam, salvation must mean the reversal of Adam's loss. Man is restored by Christ's recapitulation of Adam. But sometimes Irenaeus interprets this in terms of Christ's human obedience by which Adam's disobedience is reversed and annulled, and sometimes, on the other hand, in terms of the union of humanity in the Incarnation with the immortality and incorruptibility of the Son of God, who became what we are in order to make us what he is. Here we find an unresolved tension, characteristic of the Greek fathers, between salvation through participation in Christ's ethical conquest of sin and salvation through participation in the nature of the Logos. However this may be, Irenaeus holds that our union with the Logos incarnate and with his Spirit is effected through the operation of faith and love and through the sacraments. Hence Psalm 82.6, 'I said, you are gods', applies to all Christians, for they have received the spirit of adoption by which we cry, 'Abba, Father'. Perfection will come, however, only after our resurrection with the incorruptibility that is given in the vision of God.[6]

Here we encounter the typical patristic interpretation of salvation as deification, a concept which may still have much to teach us. It has often been misunderstood, and it has had a bad press among Protestant theologians, being alleged to be unbiblical, typically Eastern and related to the entire complex of distinctively Orthodox culture and spirituality, blurring the distinction between the Creator and the created, and implying a denial of salvation by grace alone, responded to and apprehended by faith alone.

In fact, however, deification, virtually equated with likeness to God, means the operation of sanctifying grace, already experienced by believers who are indwelt by God's Spirit and thereby produce the 'harvest' of love, joy, peace and the other Christlike characteristics (Gal. 5.22f.). Through grace they already enjoy communion with God, like that of sons with a Father, but the full realization of this awaits the final consummation. Although the most direct expression of the idea of deification in the New Testament is the startling description of believers as 'partakers of the divine nature' in II Peter 1.4, the scriptural basis for the patristic teaching is usually the Pauline concept of sonship by adoption and grace and of the re-creation of believers through assimilation to the likeness of Christ, the image of God. Whatever may have happened to the idea of deification in later Eastern thought (and Orthodox theologians tend to presuppose that it has always been much more uniform and static than the critical study of the fathers would allow), it is in no way inconsistent with the Pauline conception of justification by grace and faith. Nor do the fathers lose sight of the fact that the natures of uncreated deity and the human creation remain unconfused. On the contrary, the idea of deification was worked out in opposition to the Gnostic theory of a natural participation by men, or at any rate some 'spiritual' men, in God, and it was based on the central patristic understanding of the work of Christ as an interchange of places, by which the Son of God became what we are in order that we might become sons of God in him.

The fact that the Logos had to become what we are indicates that we are not by nature divine; and that men may become 'gods' is no embarrassment to the Christian convictions that God is one and that deified men are neither consubstantial with absolute deity nor entitled to the worship that belongs only to the source of deity who is God, not by participation, but by nature. Moreover, the strong emphasis laid by most of the Fathers on the resurrection of the flesh helped to prevent deification from becoming misinterpreted as absorption into the uncreated and incorporeal Godhead. In fact, in this concept of salvation, biblical theology speaks a common language with Platonism,[7] and finds a bridge, too, for communication with the other faiths whose adherents, it is now increasingly clear, no Christian doctrine may rightly treat as excluded from the sphere of salvation.

Three points in Clement of Alexandria's treatment of this theme are worth notice. The soul is created, and is not to be identified with the divine, and although assimilation to God involves the closest personal communion it does not mean absorption.[8] Secondly, although Clement thinks of salvation as the fullness of spiritual contemplation rather than as deliverance from death and corruption, he anomalously maintains the traditional biblical idea of a resurrection of the body. Thirdly, freedom from the passions (*apatheia*), by which man is set at liberty to contemplate God, is combined with love (*agape*). This is often said to indicate the difference between Christian *apatheia* and Stoic 'detachment', and there is truth in this distinction; yet here there may be another tension within early Christian ideas of salvation, for although it is recognized that the fruit of the Spirit is love, salvation, interpreted as the deification of the human soul, or the human mixture of soul and body, does tend to be thought of as a solitary process.

Hellenized Christianity, in contrast with Old Testament thought, certainly individualized the idea of salvation. There is little emphasis on the redemption and perfection of society as such. A contrast is sometimes drawn between the Christian recognition that at every stage of the ascent to God the believer must be in community and the teaching of Plotinus that the importance, first, of the political community and, later, of the community of intelligences which constitutes the visible universe diminishes as the soul approaches union with the One.[9] It is true that the Christian concept of moral perfection includes the belief that it is in one's neighbour that one meets and loves Christ. Yet for Clement, Origen and Athanasius the Christian's encounter seems really to be with the *Logos* in Christ, and indeed, for Origen it really means encounter with, and love for, the *discarnate* Logos. It is not easy to love the Logos, the source of transcendent goodness, beauty and truth, in the person of one's human neighbour, even though one must find in him the Jesus of the gospels. In fact, the ultimate state of beatitude, as envisaged by Origen or Gregory of Nyssa, seems to be an immediate and individual relationship between the soul and God. There is, and will be, a communion of saints, but for these writers heaven seems more like a concourse of individually saved souls than a redeemed society. In this respect the difference between a good deal of early Christian thought and Neoplatonism can easily be exaggerated. Augustine, however, who uses the concept of deification as extensively as any Greek theologian, supplies a certain corrective to this tendency in his insistence that men are deified through loving God, and that this love must include the human neighbour; if one human person denies humanity to another human person, God will deny him the gift of divinity by which he makes men 'gods'.[10]

The naive millenarianism of Papias, Justin and Irenaeus fell into disfavour under the influence of the spiritualizing and intellectualizing tendencies of more sophisticated eschatologies, and there is little evidence of concern in patristic theology for a redemption of the material creation. Salvation is more a saving out of this material world than a saving of it. The exception to this is belief in bodily resurrection, almost spiritualized away by Origen but maintained by Tertullian (who also held that the soul is material) in a strictly physical sense in which it was also defended by opponents of Origen's cosmology and eschatology. The belief seems anomalous if salvation is equated with deification, since God is not corporeal. It seems to have been valued as part of the scriptural tradition (though Paul's 'spiritual body' is far removed from Tertullian's *resurrectio carnis*), as a safeguard against any blurring of the ultimate distinction between Creator and creatures (though this should have been secured by the acknowledgment of the soul itself as part of the created order), and as a defence against Gnostic and Manichaean depreciation of the value of the material creation (though there seems no reason why, if the material is accorded its proper value, it should necessarily be regarded as everlasting).

More interesting and important than the idea of a resurrection of the body as such is Gregory of Nyssa's view that man, created as a synthesis of soul and body and not, as Origen held, as pure spirit, is intended by God to mediate the spiritual to the material. He has a foot in both worlds; he is the bridge between spirit and matter, and when man becomes reunited with, and assimilated to, God, the harmony of the universe, now disrupted by man's alienation from God, will be restored.[11] This idea, developed in the teaching of Maximus the Confessor that man is meant to bridge the divisions between heaven and earth, God and creation, paradise and this present state, male and female, and that in so far as man enters into union with God he will effectively realize his true nature as 'microcosm' and his function as the hinge of creation, on whom depends the proper balance of nature,[12] has much to say to modern man, perplexed by the problem of his relation to the environment. These theologians took an anthropocentric view of the universe, and in this they were in line with the Pauline teaching in Romans 8. The notion of cosmic redemption is hard to understand, and if it means anything it seems to presuppose some kind of historical Fall at the cosmic level. But nature, save for man's constant tendency to 'fall', in the sense of setting up his own selfish interests against the will of God, is presumably at the point in the evolutionary process where the Creator intends it to be. In his sight it is surely 'very good', and in itself it needs no 'redemption'. Nature, however, enslaved and despoiled by the selfishness of mankind, is certainly 'groaning' and waiting for the salvation of the human race. Indeed, if the deification of man, collectively, does not make some speedy progress, little of the rest of creation is likely to be left on this planet to greet the manifestation of mankind as sons of God. Man's relationship to nature is to transform it, for good or ill: and here Christian thought about creation and salvation has a point of contact with Marxism.

Hans Küng tells us that people today do not want to be divinized; they want rather to be fully humanized. No doubt this is true; and much that the Orthodox tradition teaches about deification has an air of unreality, and, when seen in the context of Eastern ascetical theology, of strangeness to the point of being bizarre or even repellent. Yet the fathers would not have made this sharp distinction. The likeness of God into which we are moulded is the perfection of humanity. It is God disclosed and mediated to us in Christ who is the God to whom, by grace, we are made like. In reshaping our ideas of salvation we should, no doubt, speak of humanization rather than divinization, for people do want to become truly human, not to be godlike; but Christians go on from there to affirm that to be fully human is to be Christlike, and this is what the ancient theologians themselves seem to have thought.

It seems that the early church's hopes for salvation were generally deficient in their social implications. Men thought they were saved out of the world into the church and through the church into an eschatological kingdom of heaven, with little idea of a salvation of human society and a transformation of its structures according to God's will. Partly this was due to an eschatological perspective which never really ceased to be foreshortened; salvation was thought to belong properly to the hereafter. The social and political situation of the early church meant that during its most formative years it could not combine, like Israel of old, the roles of religious and political community; hence it could not have successors to Amos and Isaiah as prophets of social justice. The idea of the new Jerusalem on earth was scarcely a substantial vision, and it soon came to be dismissed as a piece of naive literalism. So the kingdom of God was reinterpreted in terms either of heaven, after death and judgment, or of God's reign in the individual soul, or again as a partial anticipation of heaven in the 'angelic life' of the monastic communities.

We may ask in conclusion whether the great preoccupation of traditional thought about salvation with immortality may not itself look unpleasantly like an extension of human self-centredness and self-seeking: the heavenly reward, 'glory for me'. It does sometimes have this appearance. Two points, however, must be remembered. The idea of deification means that this glory is the glory of God disclosed in Christ, not the glory of man in his acquisitive nature, and the death which precedes this entry into immortality should not be identified simply with physical dying. It is rather the daily dying with Christ, the death of the Pauline 'old man', the losing of one's life to gain it, and, in the most literal and practical fashion in the early church, the sharing of Christ's death in martyrdom, for deification and martyrdom are closely linked.

3

What Future for the Trinity?

What future for the Trinity? If it meant, 'What future is there for God – God who, according to traditional trinitarian language, is the Creator, the Saviour, and the Sanctifier?', it could perhaps be answered in quite a few words. In a sense the future that there is for God is all the future that there is; for there is no future for ourselves or for any other part of his created universe, except in so far as we receive it from him in total dependence on his sustaining providence. At the same time many theists would want to say that in his own being God has neither future nor past, for he is unchanging and transcends the time process.

But of course the question we are asking is what future is there for the traditional, classical, *doctrine* of the Trinity, I am bound to reply, even within these walls of Trinity College, 'Not much'. But in saying this I want to keep very much in mind the distinction between doctrines and faith: that is, between 'the Faith' and 'faith'. Faith is a response of belief, commitment and trust that may be evoked from us by our experience. Doctrines are more or less sophisticated theological propositions which we construct in order to articulate our faith, to clarify its contents and significance, to relate it to other aspects of our total outlook on life, and to enable us to give a rational account of it both to ourselves and to other people. By bringing these theological formulations into relation with each other and establishing the connections between them we may be able to build them into a coherent system of thought: 'the Faith'. But they are always more or less tentative and provisional. They are models constructed so as to help us towards some kind of understanding of a reality, the object of our faith, which necessarily eludes literal precise, or exhaustive description. For this reality itself always lies beyond the grasp of our finite minds.

These conceptual models that we call doctrines are in some respects similar to the models with which the scientist operates, though the religious believer, the person who has faith, uses them, not to make prediction possible, but to illustrate and articulate the insights of faith. The doctrine of the Trinity is one such model. If, in changing circumstances, a particular doctrine ceases to serve this purpose effectively, it may come to be modified, or gradually transferred from the centre of the Faith to the periphery, or even discarded and replaced by some other model. But because Christian theology is not an activity of individual thinkers only but also of a community of believers (the *faithful*), a doctrinal model may at any given time continue to be valued and cherished by some, while others find it unsatisfactory and are seeking to modify or replace it. When divine revelation was believed to be given us directly in terms of propositions, that is, when it was believed that there are revealed doctrines, carrying God's timeless authority, each of these two groups of believers identified its own model with orthodoxy and that of the others with heresy. So the classical statement of the doctrine of the Trinity, the so-called Athanasian Creed, ends: 'This is the Catholick Faith: which except a man believe faithfully he cannot be saved.' This has been paraphrased in less dignified language: 'Accept my model or I'll do you', or rather, 'This is God's model: accept it or he will do you', to which a distressingly large number of Christians in the past were eager to add, 'and I am ready to act as God's agent.' But divine revelation does not come to us packaged into doctrines. It is given to us, rather, in that scarcely definable but yet quite undeniable sense of encountering the transcendent: of experiencing our finite, small-scale, existence in a perspective, or within a dimension, that transcends its limitation. If our cultural inheritance includes the concepts and the language of theism, we interpret that awareness of transcendence as a sense of being encountered by God. It may take many forms: transcendent beauty, goodness, love, and it may be mediated through many different forms of experience: aesthetic, intellectual, personal. For Christians – and this is what is distinctive in Christianity – the central and culminating point in all these many and varied disclosures of a divine dimension in human life is the person of Jesus, as understood and interpreted by the

---

people of the New Testament and by subsequent generations of believers. Through him they have experienced the possibility of a relationship to God grounded in God's spontaneous and unmerited love and in a human response of trust and commitment to God which, in turn, enables human beings to become a channel of that same divine love to one another. In him they have seen the actual embodiment of that kingdom of God to which he pointed in his parables and which he made effective in his works of mercy and compassion. Man was created in God's image and likeness; Adam, man, is God's son. In Jesus there is the realization of the Creator's purpose; he is the true Adam, the Son of God, reflecting, in a human life, the nature of God himself.

From the beginning Christians used many models to articulate and express the central insight of their faith that in Jesus they encountered this perfect realization and embodiment of the union, in an authentic human life, of the divine Spirit with the spirit of man. This concept of divine Spirit, that is, God himself reaching out to the human personality, indwelling, inspiring and motivating it without violating its own autonomy, is itself one such model, and I believe it is still potentially a very valuable way of interpreting God's active presence in Jesus and in ourselves. Many others, however, were available in the early church's scriptures, that is, the Old Testament. God's people, Israel, was there spoken of as 'God's son', called to be his servant and representative to the rest of the world. Within that community the king was regarded as one who stood in a special relationship of calling, intimacy and service towards God. To him, or at any rate to the hoped-for Messiah who would one day realize in actuality the ideal concept of a true agent of God's own kingdom of peace and justice, God was pictured as saying, 'Thou art my son, this day' (namely, the day of his enthronement) 'have I begotten thee.' In Jesus that ancient hope seemed to have been translated into reality. Though far from being a king in the ordinary outward sense, he was the real Messiah, anointed with God's Spirit and power; and as such he was the Son of God. St Paul speaks of Christ, 'the wisdom of God', and St John sums up the theme of the gospel story by telling us that 'the word was made flesh and dwelt among us'. 'Wisdom' and 'word' are models taken from the Old Testament. They convey the idea of God's creative purpose and his communication of it to his rational creation. And if men found in Jesus a supreme

communication of the mind and character and creative will of
God, then Jesus was not just another prophet (though they did
call him a prophet) to whom the word of God had been spoken;
he was a personal embodiment of God's address to us; he was
God's word or wisdom or spirit (in Hebrew wisdom writings
those three terms are synonymous) incarnate.

With this concept of Jesus as God's personal communication
to mankind in and through the life of a human person there
came, however, to be combined a different model. The concepts
of word and wisdom and spirit had been evolved to express the
human experience of being touched and moved and inspired
by God. Under the influence, especially, of Platonist thought
they came to be used to answer such questions as: 'How can
transcendent deity be related to this material world, and impassible deity be concerned with, and intervene in, the processes of history?' 'How can unchanging deity be involved in
the constant flux of an ever-changing world of generation and
dissolution without himself becoming subject to change?' 'How
is the absolute one-ness of God related to the many, the manifold and composite universe of his creation?' Such questions
gave rise to the model of word and wisdom as personified
attributes and almost as intermediary beings, not other than
God in their essence but nevertheless subordinate agents of
God, serving both as lines of communication through which
God acts upon the temporal world indirectly and at the same
time as fenders or buffers between it and his own transcendent,
timeless, impassible being. So for the Alexandrian Jewish Platonist, Philo, the word (Logos) is God's pre-existing agent in
creation, his firstborn Son, his perfect image, containing in
himself the archetypal ideas or forms which are the blueprint,
as it were, for the manifold universe. In the Wisdom of Solomon, which comes from the same background as Philo, and
earlier in the book of Proverbs, wisdom is poetically imagined
as God's companion and helper, executing his creative purpose
and communicating his mind to his human creatures.

So the way was open, once the Christian experience of meeting God in Jesus had been articulated in terms of these concepts,
for the process of personification to be completed. If Jesus is
seen as the incarnation of God's word, and if the word is taken
to mean Philo's Logos, then the Logos is, and always was,
Jesus. The personal identity of Jesus is projected back on to the
pre-existent Logos. He is no longer Son of God in the sense in

which Adam, Israel, and the Messiah are Son of God; he is God
the Son: a quite different model. The historical figure of Jesus
is God the Son; he came down to earth from heaven – and, as
Christian creeds want to go on to say, he was made man. But
the model of the pre-existent Logos/Son has always proved
extraordinarily difficult – many would say impossible – to re-
concile with the assertion of the genuine manhood of the historical Jesus.

Nor was that model at first satisfactory for articulating the
faith of Christians that God himself, in the fullness of his being,
finds them in and through Jesus. To identify Jesus with the
Logos/Son seemed for a time to solve many problems. It made
it possible to say that Jesus is God; yet to avoid the scandalous
paradox of admitting that God in the sense of ultimate and
absolute deity was born and suffered and died. The subject of
the experiences recorded in the gospels was God; but not God
the Father. It was the Son, the Logos who is not different from
God the Father but is yet distinct from him, so that he can even
be called, as he was by Philo, 'second God'. He is the mediator
between God and the world, a kind of two-way mirror, reflecting God downwards, as it were, to the created universe and
reflecting the world upwards to God. Yet the logic of the basic
Christian experience of meeting God in Jesus compelled the
church, when Arius asserted that the Son is not only distinct
but different from God, and thus forced the choice upon it, to
opt for the creed of Nicaea and the model of the Logos, God
the Son, who is of the same substance or essence as the Father.
In the end this meant a total identification of the Son with the
Father: 'Such as the Father is, such is the Son.' The distinction
is solely in their mode of subsistence: 'The Father,' says the
Athanasian Creed, 'is made of none: neither created nor begotten.' So a model which had been developed to make it possible
to claim that Jesus is God, and yet to deny that God is Jesus,
simply and, as it were, without remainder leads to the theological puzzle of two distinct entities, 'persons' (in the sense of
entities without the modern psychological connotations of the
word 'person') absolutely one and the same in all respects save
that the one is a projection of the other, eternally generated
from the other yet without any other difference whatsoever. I
believe that had Christians in the beginning adopted a model
of inspiration to express their experience of deity in Jesus, and
spoken of him as a man totally moved and inspired by God

(indeed, by God's spirit, wisdom or word, so long as these are not personified as distinct divine beings), they could have claimed for Jesus what their faith demanded without their doctrine running out into meaninglessness.

At the same time Christian faith was experiencing God as a continuing personal presence, interacting with the spirit of man, inspiring, moving, renewing, representing the character of Christ in a community so motivated by his spirit (the spirit of God that was in him) that it could be called the body of Christ, recreating the individual human personality after the pattern of Christ, that is, in the image and likeness of God. It would have been possible to express this experience in terms of 'word' or 'wisdom', but these had largely come to be pre-empted to interpret the Christian understanding of Jesus. It was therefore that other Old Testament model, the spirit of God or holy spirit, which was used to articulate the continuing experience of God in the life of the community, in the many and various charismata which enriched its life, and above all in the distinctive Christ-like quality of self-giving love. 'Holy spirit' language was used in order to speak of God, Creator and Saviour, interacting with the minds and feelings of human beings in such a way as to make them sons of God, 'sanctifying' them – which means making them his own people.

It was a comparatively long time before theologians turned their attention directly to the metaphysical question of the nature of the reality to which this 'holy spirit' language pointed. It was in the fourth century that the orthodox doctrine of the deity of the Holy Spirit was finally worked out. Quite rightly it maintained that when we speak of the Holy Spirit we mean no less than God himself: not an impersonal force or influence, not a subordinate, created, personal power such as an angel. Less happily, I think, it was not content to say that the Spirit is God; it asserted the doctrine of a third 'person' of the deity. Yet it soon proved impossible to distinguish this entity from the other two, either in function or in any other respect save, once again, in his mode of being. This presented a theological problem. If the Spirit was neither made nor begotten he would be a second ingenerate principle: there would be two Fathers. If he was begotten, there would be two Sons. If he was made, he would be a creature and not a God. Verbally the problem was solved by using the Johannine term 'proceed': 'neither made, nor created, nor begotten, but proceeding'. But when John spoke of the Spirit proceeding from the Father he meant 'coming from God to the world, to ourselves'. The fourth-century theologians took this term out of its New Testament setting and applied it to the quite different context of the metaphysical problem of the ontology of the third person: God the Spirit. And the orthodox doctrine was and is that God the Spirit is distinct from the Father and the Son in respect of, and only in respect of, the fact that he is the same God in the mode of procession and not in the mode of generation or sonship nor in the mode of ingeneracy. It is, I think, a sign that the models have somehow been misused that no one has ever ventured to suggest what the difference is between generation and procession.

For trinitarian orthodoxy is often misunderstood. As set out in the Athanasian Creed, which for this purpose is authoritative, the doctrine is that there are three persons, distinguished only by their mode of subsistence, each of whom is otherwise identical with each of the others and with the whole triad. If we speak of a relationship of love between the divine persons we must be clear that this is the love of God for himself: and St Augustine, when he spoke of this relationship as that of lover, loved one, and the bond of love uniting them, was quite clear that he was trying to say something about God's self-contemplation and self-love. It is sometimes said that the doctrine of the Trinity answers the question how God could be eternally the God of love if he had not from all eternity a created universe as the object of his love; but I do not think that the all-sufficiency of God implies a distinction of 'persons' within his being. Most popular expositions of the Trinity tend to be tritheistic: and tritheism is impossible for those who believe in the infinity of God, for there cannot be more than one infinite personal being.

I believe we should rethink the use of doctrinal models which led to the formulation of this doctrine – but not the faith which they are intended to express. If we do substitute unitarianism for trinitarianism it must not be the unitarianism that denies the divinity of Christ. On the contrary, I believe we can assert that God was in Christ, without using the model of 'God the Son'. It must not be a unitarianism which postulates a deistically-conceived God remote from the world, separated from our human hearts and minds; we must acknowledge the present reality of God with us and in us; yet without, I hope, the confusions of the fourth-century theology of the Holy Spirit. We have to preserve and safeguard the reality of Christian experience and faith; but there is room to try to find fresh forms of theological expression for it.

4

A Sermon for Trinity Sunday

This morning's first reading, from Isaiah 6.1–8, brings us into touch with an ancient Hebrew prophet as a real live person – an actual individual. This is something which does not often happen in the prophetic literature. But here a man who lived in Jerusalem in the eighth century before Christ tells us something about his own personal life-story, directly and in the first person.

'In the year that King Uzziah died,' he begins, as if he were telling some ordinary anecdote. We might expect him to go on: 'In the year that King Uzziah died I moved house,' or 'I started work in such and such a business.' What he actually says is: 'In the year that King Uzziah died I saw the Lord.' It's the sort of statement that would make it difficult to keep a conversation going, the kind of remark which would make one think the speaker was an exceedingly odd person, perhaps even a dangerous oddity. But this man, Isaiah of Jerusalem, follows up that extraordinary statement with a detailed account of his vision. For he had seen a vision in the temple. It was a vision of the glory of God, a vision of the seraphim, heavenly beings, crying to one another in those words which became part of our Christian liturgy: 'Holy, holy, holy is the Lord of hosts: the whole earth is full of his glory.'

The effect of the vision on Isaiah is a classical, archetypal, instance of an experience of conversion and calling. It has often been repeated from those far-off days down to the present time – a sense of his own falsity and unreality in face of divine holiness and beauty (for I take that to be Isaiah's meaning when he said, 'I am a man of unclean lips, and I dwell in the midst of a people of unclean lips' – lips unable to speak the truth); he felt himself to be a sham person, destroyed by the vision of God's reality – a sense of being reached out to, touched, and purified; the coal from the altar has touched his lips and his 'iniquity is taken away and his sin purged' – a sense, finally, of being called: 'I heard the voice of the Lord, saying, "Whom shall I send, and who will go for us?" Then I said, "Here am I, send me." ' He found in himself this deep conviction that he must prophesy. He must speak God's word to the nation: 'Go, and tell this people' – even though he knew already, in the very moment of this overpowering conviction, that the people would never listen. We know what the content of his message was, for we can read it in the chapters that precede and follow this story. Israel, the vineyard planted by the Lord, had turned sterile and useless, fit only to be broken down and laid waste, because God's righteousness demanded social justice, and all that the nation produced was exploitation and oppression.

'I saw the Lord,' says Isaiah. Yet St John is right when he tells us that 'no man has seen God at any time'. God is not a finite object, to be seen by human eyes or grasped by the human mind. God does not speak to us or touch us directly, but always through the medium of our human experience, through human ideas and emotions and imagination. Many forms of our experience may sometimes turn out to be channels of God's communication with us; sometimes it is in the most ordinary things that happen to us that we find God – or God finds us. Isaiah's vision was quite evidently made up of elements of his own familiar experience. He was in the temple; the seraphim were apparently carved flying serpents or something of the kind, guarding the 'mercy seat', the lid of the holy ark, which was believed to be the locus of the presence of the invisible God. 'The house was filled with smoke', presumably of incense and sacrifices. The hymn, 'Holy, holy, holy is the Lord' would be suggested by the temple psalms; in fact, Psalm 72 ends with the words, 'Let the whole earth be filled with his glory.' The temple was the king's chapel, as it were, built by Solomon, and the imagery in which Isaiah pictured the presence of God is that of a king, high and lifted up; his train filled the temple. So at that moment of revelation the building and its furnishings and the liturgy all came alive in Isaiah's imagination, and spoke to him of God's glory and his own calling. It does not make God's word any the less real when we recognize that it is always mediated through the human, in terms of our various cultures and traditions and intellectual presuppositions. Unless, perhaps, we had soaked ourselves in the thought of the Old Testament, none of us nowadays would see God in the imagery which was appropriate for Isaiah.

This reminds us that all the images and all the forms of thought which may be modes of revelation to human beings are at best transient and inadequate. To suppose that religious imagery, liturgical patterns, or theological formulations are more than aids to our understanding, to confuse them with the divine reality itself, is idolatry. An idol is a god created in the image of men, a god who can be comfortably and comfortingly controlled and manipulated by human individuals and human societies. But the true God can never be grasped or pinned down or harnessed. That is what it means to say that God is infinite and incomprehensible. 'No man has seen God at any time.' That is why in the Old Testament the 'name' of God is the undefined, open-ended, 'I am', or, as it may be better translated, 'I will be what I will be'. You cannot predict what God will be; you can only discover something of what God will be as life goes on and God goes on communicating acceptance, love and hope in mysterious, and generally very unexpected, ways.

A word much used in the Hebrew and Christian traditions for speaking about God is 'Spirit'. This is a very vague term, and partly for that reason it is a most useful one. The basic concept which underlies it in most languages, though less clearly so in English, is that of 'wind' or 'breath'. It suggests that God inspires, breathes life, animates his creatures. It implies that God's outreach to us and his action upon us are somehow not unlike the way the wind blows. 'The wind bloweth where it listeth,' we are told in this morning's Gospel, 'and thou hearest the sound thereof, but canst not tell whence it cometh nor whither it goeth.' You cannot see the actual wind itself. You cannot grasp the wind. You can see its effects; you can feel its power. You may take some action on your side to bring yourself into line, so to speak, with that power, such as hoisting a sail or putting up a windmill. And taking that sort of action, attaching yourself, as it were, to the wind or spirit that is God, and so enabling yourself and other people to be driven by it in the direction in which it is going, is, roughly speaking, what openness to God, or prayer, seems to mean. Electricity might offer another analogy: to become open to God is rather like bringing an electric train into contact with an overhead wire or a third rail. But electricity is artificially generated: the wind is uncontrolled, and unpredictable in its effects, like God whom we call Spirit.

We cannot make a picture of the wind itself; we cannot make a true image of God. Properly speaking, I suppose it might be better not to use the personal pronoun to refer to God, and it may be wise of my Cambridge colleague, Don Cupitt, in his recent writings always to repeat the word 'God', and never to speak of God as 'he'. Yet, on the other hand, our experience of God is analogous to our experience of human persons. We can use the language of human relationship – love, compassion, care, justice, and so on – to speak of our awareness of God; indeed, it is so often *in* those human relationships that we come to have glimpses of the divine, as a kind of extra dimension: a transcendent love, care, forgiveness, compassion. And these relationships are essentially personal. The analogy of the wind or of electric current must not be pressed so as to imply that God is like an impersonal force, and nothing more. So we may do well, after all, to use the personal pronoun, always, of course, remembering, as many people find it difficult to do because of our cultural inheritance, that the pronoun is equally 'he' or 'she', no more the one than it is the other. It is with this proviso that we may use the analogy of an intimate personal relationship and speak of 'God the Father'.

We must not try to make an image of God. But God, we believe, has made an image of himself. 'God created man in his own image, in the image of God created he him; male and female created he them.' We are God's image, or, at any rate, that is what we are intended to become. It is what we are made for. God takes a long time to make a human being, as David Attenborough has reminded us. Millions of years go into that process. And the creation of human beings who reflect the likeness of Isaiah's God, who requires justice and mercy and truth in the relationships of human society, is a peculiarly long and difficult business. For the Creator is working on mysteriously recalcitrant material, and the process of creating human beings as personal souls seems to be carried out through the inward interaction of personal God with personal creatures. It seems to be a creation through personal approach and personal response, a creation to which the creative processes of education may give us some kind of analogy or clue – and the human response is always poor, and often actually hostile.

We believe that the goal of this gradual and painful creative process has been reached – by anticipation: that in Jesus the real Adam has actually appeared on the human scene, within the history of man's evolution – man made in the image of God, man in the full perfection of that mutual interaction between the divine and the human. Here is God, transcendent love and truth and goodness and compassion, disclosed in a human being. Here, too, in this same person, there is disclosed the model and archetype of our humanity as God intends it to be, freely responding to, and reflecting, transcendent deity: man as God's son, the firstborn, as New Testament writers put it, of many brothers – of all men, transformed by God's Spirit into Christlikeness, created, or re-created, in his image.

God who can never be comprehended or defined; God who, nevertheless, shows us his human reflection in Jesus; God creating us in the pattern of Jesus by his personal interaction with ourselves – beyond all the Platonist metaphysics of traditional trinitarian doctrine, which say little, I think, to us today, this is the focus of our Trinity Sunday worship.

5

The Two Swords
(Luke 22.38)

'This record of Jesus' arming of his disciples, or rather his checking on their armament,' remarks S. G. F. Brandon, 'has greatly troubled commentators.'[1] The idea that in Luke 22.36–38 Jesus is acting like an officer 'checking on' his men's weapons is bizarre indeed; but that the commentators on Luke have floundered in a morass of perplexity when faced by this notoriously difficult passage is certainly true. Brandon can cite examples of the diverse and sometimes contradictory explanations which have been offered by exegetes, who have tried rather desperately to establish the meaning, or, rather, to make any sense at all, of this strange pericope. I have to admit that they include myself, in *Peake's Commentary*. Their embarrassment has not been caused by the misuse of the passage in the Middle Ages as a scriptural basis for theories concerning the relations between the Papacy and the Empire. It is due, rather, to the obscurity which made it possible for such a fantastic interpretation to appear plausible.

The first question to be considered is the relation of Luke 22.38 ('And they said, "Lord, see, here are two swords." And he said, "It is enough" '), on the one hand to the preceding dialogue in vv. 35–37, and on the other to Luke's version (in vv. 49–51) of the Marcan episode of the assault on the servant of the high priest (Mark 14.47; Matt. 26.51–54; John 18.10f.). As this verse stands, in its context in Luke, it is evidently intended to form part of the dialogue which precedes it (vv. 35–37), and is itself an integral part of the warnings, instruction and promises given by Jesus at the Last Supper. This is a section of Luke which resembles on a small scale, and, as it were, prepares the way for the great Johannine discourses at and after the Supper.

Yet it does not seem to be logically connected with this material. If it was originally part of the dialogue which precedes it, we must suppose either that it was intended to express the disciples' lack of comprehension and their insensitivity both to the true significance of Jesus' words and to the situation that evoked them, or that Luke has clumsily added it to the dialogue between Jesus and the disciples in vv. 35–37, with the object of establishing a connection between this and the episode of the attack upon the high priest's servant.

Several distinct units of tradition have apparently been brought together by Luke into relationship with one another. These are: (1) the instructions given to the Seventy when they were sent out on their mission (10.3ff.), with the parallel commissioning of the Twelve (9.3ff.); (2) the warning to the disciples that the times have changed and that their original instructions have now to be countermanded (22.35–37); (3) the saying of the disciples concerning two swords and Jesus' reply to them (22.38); (4) the Marcan episode of the attack on the servant of the high priest, preceded by the disciples' question, 'Lord, shall we strike with the sword?', and followed by the healing of the servant's ear by Jesus (22.49–51).

At 10.3f. Jesus sends out the Seventy, ordering them not to carry purse or bag or sandals. This passage is broadly, but not exactly, paralleled in Mark 6.8f. and Matt. 10.9f., followed also by Luke 9.3f., where the instruction is given to the Twelve. The source criticism of this passage is complicated; it is possible that in this material there is an overlap between Mark and Q, and perhaps with L as well. However this may be, it is likely that Luke has taken material which in his source referred to the sending out of the Twelve and inserted it in the new context of the commissioning of the Seventy. This passage is taken up at 22.35f. Here Jesus addresses the Twelve and reminds them how they were originally sent out, without purse, bag or sandals. It may be that Luke is himself confused, and has forgotten that he had transferred the instructions of Jesus to the Twelve into his new context of the sending out of the Seventy. But it is more probable that in Luke's source, which Vincent Taylor may be right in assigning to the L material,[2] the groundwork of vv. 35–37 was already associated with the substance of 10.3f.; both referred to the sending of the Twelve. The problem of the sources of vv. 35–38 has been minutely studied by H. Schürmann,[3] as well as by Vincent Taylor and others. It seems probable that vv. 35–37, or even 35–38, are a Lucan redaction of source material and were already, in the pre-Lucan stage of the tradition, linked with 10.3f. as well as with the farewell discourses of Jesus at the Last Supper (22.21–34).

Jesus reminds his disciples that when he originally sent them out they were without even the ordinary basic requirements for a journey. He asks them whether they had lacked anything, and their answer, 'Nothing', presumably implies that in the successful mission (10.17f.) they had been well received; they had found 'sons of peace' to receive their greeting and the 'hire' which they deserved as 'workers' (10.5–8). *But now* (22.36) the situation has drastically changed. In the scheme of successive epochs which Conzelmann discerns in Luke this phrase, ἀλλὰ νῦν, plays a decisively important role. It inaugurates a new period, in which the disciples begin once again to be assailed by trials and temptations (πειρασμοί) after a time of immunity during Jesus' ministry.[4] It is very doubtful whether this saying, or similar 'epochal' turning-points on which Conzelmann's exegesis of Luke depends, will bear the weight which his theory places on them. Within somewhat narrower limits of interpretation, however, the contrast expressed in Luke's ἀλλὰ νῦν does signify the dramatic change that is going to come in the lives of the disciples. Whereas they had been popular preachers and healers, able to count on public support wherever they went, the time is coming when no one will help them. They will have to fend for themselves; they will need purse and bag, and since every man's hand will be against them to the point of actually threatening their lives, each of them will need to arm himself with a sword even at the cost, if necessary, of selling his cloak to buy it.

A small point may be worth noticing. It has often been pointed out that in Matthew's version of the Q material found at Matt. 5.40//Luke 6.29 the cloak (ἱμάτιον), which served the peasant as a kind of sleeping-bag, is the most necessary garment of all, which a man would be most loath to surrender (cf. Ex. 22.26f., LXX). In Luke's version, however, the order is reversed, as though one would give up one's cloak sooner than one's tunic (χιτών). In this saying, however, the need to buy a sword is so pressing that it demands even the sacrifice of the cloak itself. Perhaps this is yet another indication to add to Schürmann's evidence that this pericope belongs to pre-Lucan literary tradition and is not a Lucan composition.

This passage (vv. 35–37) falls into an easily recognized category of the sayings of Jesus: future or eschatological warnings of tribulation, distress and persecution, which naturally tend, as often in the New Testament, to be uttered in the context of a leave-taking (cf. Acts 20.29–31). Jesus' warning that his disciples will have to face a hostile world, shunned, boycotted, and in danger of physical assault, is in line with parts of the farewell discourses in the Fourth Gospel such as John 15.18–21 and 16.1–4, with the prophecies of persecution in the eschatological discourses such as Mark 13.9–13 and parallels (especially 'You will be hated by all men for my name's sake', Mark 13.13; Matt. 24.9; Luke 21.17), and the saying contained in the Q material at Matt. 10.34ff.//Luke 12.51ff., which warns of coming division and strife within households and families. The last of these passages is particularly interesting. Whereas in Matthew's version of it Jesus says, 'I have not come to bring peace but a sword (μάχαιραν)', in Luke's version he says, 'Do you think that I came to give peace on the earth? No, I tell you, but rather division (διαμερισμόν).' It may well be the case that Luke has deliberately altered the original form of the saying. It is unlikely that he did this through fear that the striking metaphor of a 'sword' would be interpreted literalistically to imply that Jesus intended to foment civil war; Luke is not sensitive to possibilities of misunderstanding of this sort, as Brandon points out.[5] More probably, Luke has altered the wording in order to apply the saying more exactly to the actual experience of the early church in times of persecution, and perhaps also because he has reserved the language of Jesus relating to a sword for the passage we are now considering. In this saying (22.36), the idea of a sword expresses not, as in Matt. 10.34, the disruption which conversion to Christianity will bring to the closely-knit family ties which characterized both Jewish and Graeco-Roman society, but the total hostility which disciples will encounter. Every man's hand will be against them.

This is a warning that the future tribulation such as was described in 21.17 is now imminent. It is expressed in the vivid, not to say violent, pictorial imagery that is characteristic of the eschatological predictions in the gospels and the farewell warnings elsewhere in the New Testament (Acts 20.29; II Tim. 3.1–9; II Peter 3.3ff.; cf. Luke 17.31–37; 21.18–28). The command of Jesus that any of his disciples who does not already possess a sword should go the length of selling his cloak to buy one need not be taken literally. Indeed, to do so would perhaps be as inappropriate as to try to press the details of the eschatological warnings given at 17.31ff., and to ask how a man could escape a universal catastrophe by fleeing from his housetop, or why the disaster should engulf one of two most intimate companions and leave the other to survive. The violent language is meant to convey one clear picture: whereas the disciples had once been made welcome everywhere they went, now each must be prepared for a lonely struggle to survive in a bitterly hostile world; no one will henceforth provide him with food or shelter and he will be in constant danger of assault.

Jeremias argues that, as an unfulfilled eschatological proph- ecy, v. 36 belongs to very ancient and authentic tradition.[6] This, however, raises far-reaching questions about the nature of the eschatological sayings in the synoptic gospels as a whole. More directly, it leads to the question of the relationship of vv. 35f. to the saying in v. 37 and to the rest of Luke's Last Supper discourses. In v. 37 Jesus gives two related explanations of the reason for the drastic change in the situation of his followers. First, he is himself to suffer the fate prophesied in Isa. 53.12, 'He was reckoned with transgressors.' Jeremias interprets this to mean that Jesus is to be cast out of the community of Israel as a transgressor (ἄνομος), this being the cause of the coming boycott of his followers. The form in which the prophecy is cited, μετὰ ἀνόμων ἐλογίσθη, is closer to the Hebrew than to the LXX, which reads ἐν τοῖς ἀνόμοις . . . Since Luke usually follows the LXX, this departure from that text has persuaded Schürmann and others that the citation is an integral part of the pre-Lucan material of which vv. 35f. consist. While this is very possible, it would, however, be rash to assume that it is necessarily the case. This part of the fourth 'Servant Song' was current in the early church in various forms: I *Clement* 16.13, for example, gives it as τοῖς ἀνόμοις ἐλογίσθη, and it is by no means certain that the citation in v. 37 is not the work of Luke himself rather than his source.

The quotation is followed by a second explanation of the reason why the disciples must now expect tribulation: τὸ περὶ ἐμοῦ τέλος ἔχει.

The meaning of this is ambiguous. Vincent Taylor approves of the interpretation given by Klostermann, 'My life draws to its end.'[7] Robert Eisler, however, maintains that τέλος ἔχει refers not to the end of Jesus' life, but to the fulfilment of his destined role; and the meaning could be: 'The destiny prophesied for me is being fulfilled.'[8] In either case, whether the sense of τέλος is primarily that of 'end' or 'fulfilment' – and the two possible meanings may be intentionally combined – the question arises whether this sentence is meant, in effect, to repeat and to some extent clarify Jesus' application to himself of Isa. 53.12, or whether it is a second, independent, explanation of the coming tribulation. If the latter seems more probable, the question arises whether, at the pre-Lucan stage of the tradition, the saying may perhaps have read: '. . . let him buy a sword. For my life draws to its end' (and then you will be left alone to fend for yourselves). In that case the introduction of the reference to Isa. 53.12 may have been due to Luke's redaction. According to this view of the matter, Luke may have introduced the citation from Isaiah in order to explain the phrase, τὸ περὶ ἐμοῦ τέλος ἔχει, which he found in his source, and thereby produced the rather clumsy and ambiguous juxtaposition of δεῖ τελεσθῆναι ἐν ἐμοί and τὸ περὶ ἐμοῦ τέλος ἔχει. Why Luke should have done this must be considered later. For the present we must attend to Luke's placing of vv. 35–37.

Schürmann believes that the whole pericope, vv. 35–38, already belonged in the pre-Lucan stage of the tradition to a farewell discourse at the Last Supper. This may be so, but it is by no means certain. Verses 35–37 seem to be a piece of tradition relating to the future lot of the disciples, rather than to the Passion story. Schürmann associates it also with those passages in the New Testament which reflect early Christian interest in the apostles' mission and how they and other ministers in the apostolic church maintained themselves while engaged in it; these include Luke 10.1; Acts 20.33; I Cor. 9.3ff., 13; Gal. 6.6; and I Tim. 5.17. This is no doubt correct, but Schürmann goes on to make a highly questionable assertion: that the maintenance of ministers from the church's common funds or at the common table was a matter closely related to the early Christians' common meals, and that the passage we are considering was therefore appropriately located, even at a pre-Lucan stage of the tradition, in the context of the farewell speeches of Jesus at the Supper table. But as a prophecy of future tribulation it may, rather have belonged originally to the eschatological material which Luke collected in the discourses in chs. 17 and 21. Luke, however, has placed it in the context of a series of warnings and promises which Jesus gives to the disciples at the Last

Supper. It forms the last of four units of dialogue. Their themes are Christ's covenanted promises to his disciples (22.17–19a, 29), and prophetic warnings of their treachery (Judas), denial (Peter), and, in the particular slant which Luke gives to the prophecy of Isaiah, lawless conduct: they are now to be transgressors with whom Jesus is to be reckoned. The treachery of Judas in its relation to the predetermined fate of the Son of man (22.21f.), the disciples' quarrel about greatness in its relation to the covenanting to them, as participants in Jesus' πειρασμοί, of a table in his kingdom and thrones of judgment over Israel, the prediction of Peter's denial in its relation to the promise of his restoration and future leadership, and the saying about buying a sword in its relation to the prophecy of Isa. 53.12, all have to do, according to Luke, with events that are to occur in the immediate future, when the hour of Jesus' enemies and the power of darkness are to be manifested in the garden.

Luke, it would seem, has taken the prophecy of the future plight of the disciples; he has either added to it the citation of Isa. 53.12 or, if this prophecy was already included in the pericope at an earlier stage, he has given it a new meaning. Whereas it had meant, if it was already part of this passage, that Jesus was to be cast out from Israel as a lawbreaker, Luke understands it to mean that the disciples have become transgressors and that Jesus is to be numbered with them. He conveys this meaning, in the first instance, by setting this pericope in the context of this series of promises and warnings which reveal the apostles, Jesus' followers, as unrighteous and lawless men: one is to betray the Lord, one is to deny him, all, even in the setting of the covenant supper and the predicted betrayal by one of their own number, quarrel about which of them seems to be great. All of them are ἄνομοι because they are armed, or are going to arm themselves, with swords and resort to the use of the sword in the garden. Luke has thus imposed a quite new meaning on the old saying about buying a sword. He has done this, first, by either introducing the citation of Isa. 53.12 himself, or putting it in a new setting and giving it a new reference; secondly, by either adding the dialogue about two swords (v. 38) or, again, so using it as to give it a new significance; and, thirdly, by relating the whole pericope to the preceding warnings and prophecies of treachery and failure on the part of the disciples, and also to the episode of the attack on the high priest's servant which is to be narrated in vv. 49–51.

Verse 38 records the disciples' answer to Jesus' prophecy of his own fate and their abandonment to their own devices; 'And they said, "Lord, see, here are two swords." And he said to them, "It is enough" (ἱκανόν ἐστιν).' This dialogue may conceivably have formed part of the whole pericope in a pre-Lucan stage of the literary tradition. If so, it must be understood as an inept comment by Jesus' followers on his vivid picture of their coming need to equip themselves with purse, bag, and above all sword. They catch only his 'surface meaning',[9] and suppose him not only to be talking literally about procuring swords but to be telling them to go out and buy them on the spot. Such a reaction on the part of the disciples would certainly be in line with the incomprehension and insensitivity which Luke makes them show in their response to Jesus' warnings (e.g. at 17.37 and 18.28) and, in particular, to his prophetic utterances at the Supper concerning the betrayal and Peter's denial (22.23ff., 33). More probably, however, v. 38 is Luke's own composition, for the vocabulary and style are Lucan and the verse raises notoriously difficult problems if it is taken as an integral part of a pre-Lucan pericope consisting of vv. 35–38. These include the provenance and purpose of these swords which the disciples happened to be carrying at the Last Supper, the reason why they had neither more nor fewer than two of them, and the meaning of Jesus' words, 'It is enough'. It presents fewer difficulties if it is recognized to be a Lucan addition to the traditional material contained in vv. 35–37, inserted, perhaps together with the citation of Isa. 53.12, in order to bring Jesus' warning about the need for his disciples to have a sword into relation with the episode of the high priest's servant (vv. 49–51). The preceding prophecies of Jesus concerning Judas' treachery and Peter's denial were shortly afterwards fulfilled in the garden and the high priest's house. Luke understands this traditional prophecy about the need to buy a sword as a similar 'short-term' warning which was also to be fulfilled in the garden. Hence, by placing it in the context of the disciples' coming treachery and weakness (vv. 21–34), inserting the citation of Isa. 53.12, or at least altering its application, and adding to it the dialogue in v. 38, Luke has radically changed the significance of the prophecy about buying a sword and in so doing has created major difficulties of interpretation. For the prophecy in v. 36 could not be related to the episode in vv. 49–51 without violent adjustment and distortion. Nor does v. 38 provide anything like a smooth transition from the prophecy in v. 36 to the story in vv. 49–51 which Luke takes to be its fulfilment.

Luke's starting-point for this whole operation seems to be the incident recorded in Mark 14.47 which he has reproduced at v. 50 and to which, by the additions which he supplies in vv. 49 and 51, he gives an interpretation of his own. This is an armed attack by one of the disciples acting alone (v. 50). Yet the whole body of Jesus' followers (οἱ περὶ αὐτόν) are regarded by Luke as being in a sense collectively responsible for it. Luke shows this by adding to Mark's story the question 'Lord, shall we strike with the sword?' (v. 49). To Luke this violent action, from which Jesus so emphatically dissociates himself, not only by word but by miraculous action (v. 51), identifies the disciples as the ἄνομοι of Isa. 53.12. It comes, indeed, as a climax of the offences committed by, or prophesied of, the disciples at the Supper: Judas' betrayal, Peter's denial, and the quarrel about greatness which the disciples conceived in terms of the kingdoms of the world which, as Luke made more clear in his addition to Mark in the temptation story (4.6), lie under the authority of the devil – the authority of darkness which now holds sway in the garden in the 'hour' of Jesus' enemies (22.53).

In order to explain the assault in the garden in these terms Luke has to force the traditional prophecy of Jesus about a sword into line with his interpretation of Isa. 53.12, imposing a new meaning on it and connecting it with its supposed 'fulfilment' at vv. 49–51 by means of the dialogue about 'two swords' in v. 38. The latter thus has to be understood in relation, first to the story of the armed assault as Luke interpreted this, and secondly to the warning in v. 36 about the need to have a sword, as reinterpreted by Luke in the light of his application of Isa. 53.12 to that story of the assault.

Mark 14.47 tells how, after the arrest of Jesus, 'one of the bystanders drew his sword and struck the servant of the high priest and removed his ear'. The way in which this story is presented is quite extraordinary. It has no prelude and no sequel. It appears to have no connection at all with the events that precede and follow it. We are not told who this assailant was. Mark does not say that he was one of Jesus' followers; he is simply one of those anonymous bystanders who appear from time to time in Mark's Passion narrative, minor actors in the drama, brought on to the stage unintroduced and casually dismissed without any explanation of their presence on the scene.

They appear twice as interrogators of Peter (14.69f.) and once at the cross, when they say, 'See, he calls Elijah' (15.35). Lohmeyer, in his commentary on Mark,[10] thinks that the story is told from the standpoint of those who arrested Jesus, and to them one of the disciples, 'hanging about', perhaps in a state of bewilderment, would look like a bystander. But this would be a very odd way of describing one of the band of disciples of the man whom the crowd (ὄχλος) had come to arrest. The victim of the attack seems to be someone the reader can recognize and identify, for he is not just *one* of the high priest's servants but '*the* slave of the high priest'. We are not told why he was attacked. Obviously, it was not to defend Jesus from arrest, for the arrest had already been effected. It seems reasonable to infer from Mark's peculiar treatment of the episode that he saw in it a symbolical significance. No Old Testament passage seems to furnish any possible prophecy or type, though S. G. Hall[11] made an ingenious attempt to find one. He thought the story was constructed on the basis of Ps. 40.7, following a reading like Aquila's 'Ears hast thou dug for me' (ὠτία δὲ ἔσκαψάς μοι), mistranslating *kārāh ōzēn*, 'open the ear', or perhaps confusing this Hebrew verb with *kārath*, 'cut off'. But this seems both highly improbable and quite irrelevant in Mark's context. A good case, however, has been made out for the view that the significance of the incident, as Mark understands it, lies in the fact that in the person of his servant a contemptuous insult was offered to the high priest himself.[12] Mark's curious expression, 'the slave of the high priest', is significant. It is repeated by the other three evangelists. The use of the definite article, where the servant is not otherwise identified and the reader has been told nothing about him, suggests that Mark's purpose is to call special attention to his status. He is '*the* servant' of the high priest, and is thus his personal representative. An insult offered to such a person when acting as his master's agent is an insult to his master. Daube calls attention to the recognition of this kind of vicarious insult in Roman law (Gaius, *Institut*. III, 222): 'iniuria . . . domino per eum (sc. servum) fieri videtur . . . cum quid atrocius commissum fuerit quod aperte in contumeliam domini fieri videtur, veluti si quis alienum servum verberavit', and also to the biblical examples of such conduct at II Sam. 10.4f. and in the parable of the wicked husbandmen (Mark 12.1–5).

Mark has no interest in who struck this blow, nor in what

became of him. The whole point of recording that the blow was struck is that at the very moment of the high priest's triumph, when a crowd 'from the chief priests and the scribes and the elders', as Mark specially emphasizes, has laid hands on Jesus, he receives, through his personal representative at the arrest, an injury of a peculiarly insulting and contemptuous kind. It is, moreover, an injury which if it were inflicted on him in his own person, would disqualify him for office. As Rostovtzeff pointed out, the cutting off of an ear is not likely to happen accidentally in a scuffle. It was an intentional act, done not primarily to wound, nor in a bungled attempt to kill, but to inflict on the high priest, through his representative, an indelible mark of contempt. Rostovtzeff, Lohmeyer and Daube have called attention to an Egyptian court case in which 'Hesiod cut off the right ear of Dorion' (PTebt III, 793), to penalties inflicted under Assyrian and Babylonian law, and to two close parallels to the Marcan episode: Antigonus cut off, or slit (there are variants ἀποτέμνειν or ἐπιτέμνειν) the ear of Hyrcanus II to make him unfit for the high priesthood (Josephus, *Ant.* XIV, 13.10, 366); Johanan ben Zaccai did the same to a Sadducee high priest to render him unfit to carry out a cultic service (Tosephta Parah iii.8). Mark, then, is telling us that as soon as his men had laid hands on Jesus the high priest was vicariously marked out, by the symbolic action of an unknown assailant, as disqualified from holding office. Luke adds to the Marcan story the detail that it was the right ear which was removed. John does the same, perhaps following Luke; but since John agrees with Mark against Luke in using ὠτάριον for 'ear' and ἔπαισεν for 'struck', instead of οὖς and ἐπάταξεν, while differing from both in using ἀπέκοψεν, 'cut off', instead of ἀφεῖλεν, 'removed', the precise relation between John and the synoptic traditions at this point is very difficult to determine. Luke's addition may merely be due to his fondness for vividly dramatic touches, as when he tells us that it was the right hand of the man in the synagogue that was healed (6.6, contrast Mark 3.1//Matt. 12.10). More probably, however, Luke had understood Mark's point. It was the high priest's right ear which was ceremonially smeared with the blood of the ram of consecration (Lev. 8.23f.). Luke may be interpreting the incident as a symbol, not only of the disqualification of the high priest but also of his deconsecration.

Luke, however, sees the episode in quite a different light from Mark. The high priest may have been worthy of contempt and rejection; but the armed assault on his representative was lawless aggression. We may compare Luke's treatment of the 'reviling' of the high priest by Paul at Acts 23.3–5. Both Matthew and Luke believe that Mark's unknown bystander was in fact one of the disciples. Whereas, however, in Matthew, as also in John, one disciple alone acts and is subsequently rebuked by Jesus (John naming him as Peter), Luke assigns responsibility for the assault to all the companions of Jesus, and implies that they tried to associate him with it, too. They ask, 'Lord, shall *we* strike with the sword?', and without waiting for an answer one of them strikes the servant. Only one of them strikes the blow; but the rebuke of Jesus, Ἐᾶτε ἕως τούτον, probably meaning, 'Let my enemies go so far as this (i.e., let them do even this to me)', is addressed to all the disciples. In this way Jesus immediately dissociates himself from their lawlessness. He then demonstrates his disapproval of their conduct, and his own totally different attitude, by healing the wounded man. Thus Luke shows that the disciples were rebuked and that Jesus was in no way involved, even against his will, in their lawless behaviour. In constructing this sequel to Mark's story, Luke seems to have fallen into inconsistency. He tells us that Jesus 'touched the ear and healed him'. But he has already reproduced Mark's word, ἀφεῖλεν, which means that the ear had been not merely damaged but removed. If Luke means that Jesus touched the place of the missing ear and miraculously replaced it, then this was an extraordinary healing, unparalleled in Jesus' ministry. This would certainly be an unmistakable practical demonstration of Jesus' attitude. So far as the disciples were concerned, their conduct was such as to mark them out as the ἄνομοι with whom Isaiah had foretold that the righteous Servant, himself free from ἀνομία, would be reckoned.

If Mark believed that Isaiah 53.12 referred to Jesus, he saw its fulfilment in the fact that Jesus was arrested as though he were a λῃστής ('brigand' or 'terrorist'), and was crucified with two λῃσταί (14.48; 15.27). At a later period, indeed, this seemed so obvious that a widespread but inferior reading adds after Mark 15.27, 'And the scripture was fulfilled which says, "And he was numbered with transgressors" ', evidently taking this text from Luke 22.37 and quoting it in the form in which it appears there and not directly from the LXX.

In Luke this identification is entirely absent. Jesus is arrested as though he were a λῃστής, it is true, but the two who were crucified with him are not λησταί; they are simply κακοῦργοι, 'evildoers', and Jesus is not in any way 'reckoned' with them. Luke 23.40, 'You are under the same sentence' has no bearing on this point. For Luke the transgressors are the disciples of Jesus, whose act of violent lawlessness against the high priest's representative comes after a series of predicted and actual treachery, quarrels to gain such greatness as the devil alone can give, and denial of Jesus. Luke, therefore, seeing the assault in the garden in this light, applies Isaiah's prophecy to it. He then looks for some advance warning or prophecy by Jesus of this transgression, parallel to those which he gave concerning Peter's denial and Judas' betrayal. This he finds in the tradition in the shape of the 'farewell warning' about the need to buy a sword.

The two convictions, then, on which Luke's whole construction rests are these: first, that the disciples as a body were guilty of an assault with the sword, an act of violence which Jesus rebuked in word and the effects of which he promptly repaired by a miracle; secondly, that the saying about buying a sword, with the interpretation drawn from Isa. 53.12, referred to this episode, being one of the short-term predictions and warnings delivered by Jesus at the Supper and fulfilled on the same evening. The prediction did not lend itself well to this interpretation; Luke was trying to combine and make sense of material that lay before him in Mark and in his L source, and was not writing a free composition. How could the disciples actually be expected to get hold of purses, sell cloaks, buy swords, late in the evening after the Passover feast had begun? Were they really meant to stop in the city to try to do these things on their way from the Supper to the garden? How had any of them already come to possess swords, as Jesus' words implied? This last question is if no concern to Luke. Mark had told him that a sword was used in the garden. Mark was not interested in who used it or where he had brought it from; all that mattered was that the servant's ear was removed. Luke thinks that the disciples were responsible for the attack; therefore they had at least one sword with them. Further, since their question was, 'Shall *we* strike with the sword?', the one who actually struck the blow could not have been the only disciple who had a sword. Jesus' words, ὁ μὴ ἔχων, 'he who has not a sword, let him buy one', seemed to Luke to confirm this, for they implied that some of the disciples did have swords. Luke makes the

point clear in 22.38, his own composition, as the strikingly
Lucan style shows: 'And they said, "Lord, see here are two
swords." And he said to them, "It is enough." ' In Luke's view
two swords are enough to establish the responsibility of the
disciples, to identify them collectively, and not only one individual disciple, with the ἄνομοι of Isa. 53,12 and to bring about
the fulfilment of that prophecy, possibly also to testify to their
guilt as 'two witnesses' (cf. Deut. 19.15). This is probably what
Luke intends Jesus to mean by the words ἱκανόν ἐστιν. Luke
does not consider the question how any disciples came to possess swords and, according to his reconstruction of these
events, actually brought them to the Last Supper. He is no more
interested in this than Mark was interested in why his bystander
happened to be carrying a sword. If we could cross-question
Luke about this he might well reply that the disciples had
anticipated Jesus' warning and had brought to the Supper the
instruments of their 'lawlessness', just as they had brought with
them their rivalries about worldly greatness and Judas had come
with his treachery.

It may strike us as very strange that Luke should suppose
that Jesus believed that his disciples were predestined to do
wrong, compelled to act lawlessly by a prophecy which referred
to them and must needs be fulfilled. But this, for Luke, would
only be another aspect of the great mystery focused in the
paradox which he reproduces from Mark at 22.22: 'The Son of
man is going his *appointed* way; but alas for that man by whom
he is betrayed.' Moreover, although the disciples had to become
transgressors, this did not mean that they were abandoned
without hope to the power of darkness (cf. 22.53). The very
prophecy which foretold their lawlessness said also, according
to the Hebrew text which Luke or his source seems to have
been following, that the Servant 'interceded for their transgres-
sions' (Isa. 53.12); and although 'he was led to death from' their
'lawlessnesses', they are still said at 53.8 to be 'my', that is,
God's 'people'.

If Luke has constructed his story in the light of that prophecy,
having to use some very intractable material in the process, we
need not trouble ourselves much with the many attempts to
explain 22.38 as a literal record of an actual dialogue between
Jesus and the disciples. Chrysostom supposed that the 'swords'
were really carving knives taken from the supper table where
they had been used for cutting up the Passover lamb. This

explanation has commended itself to some modern exegetes. Finlayson and Western, in a series of short articles on 'The Enigma of the Swords', suggested that the disciples had brought their fisherman's knives with them from Galilee.[13] Western thought that by ἱκανόν ἐστιν Jesus was either saying: 'These knives are large enough for all the fighting you need to do', or asking, 'Are they large enough for the fighting that you have in mind?' H. Helmbold mentions a still more eccentric explanation: the disciples had found two old swords, left over from past wars, in Peter's house at Capernaum, and brought them to defend the party from attack by Herod on their way to Jerusalem.[14] Eisler asked why, according to John 18.3, it was deemed necessary to send a whole cohort to overcome twelve men armed with only two swords. His answer was that the disciples were carrying two swords *each*, in the manner of the *sicarii* (Josephus, *Ant*. XX, 8.10, 186).[15]

None of these suggestions is in the least plausible, the last because if each disciple had attended the Supper regularly equipped as an armed *sicarius*, Jesus could not be ignorant of the fact; his comment ἱκανόν ἐστιν would then seem to express his approval; hence his words at Luke 22.35–47 become unintelligible, as does also the allusion to Isa. 53.12; and the outcome of it all in the garden would merely demonstrate that as *sicarii* the disciples were incredibly inefficient and feeble: eleven men armed with twenty-two weapons, and only one ear to show for it all.

Eisler, indeed, recognized that if the pericope of the two swords is to be used as evidence that the disciples, and perhaps Jesus himself, were militant Zealots, it has to be rewritten and transferred to a different context from the night of the betrayal. He acknowledged that Luke's framework for the saying, if this is to be interpreted on those lines, is highly implausible. In Eisler's view, τὸ περὶ ἐμοῦ τέλος ἔχει (v. 37) bore no reference to the end of Jesus' life; it indicated, rather, the completion of his purpose. The pericope, Eisler held, belongs to a time when Jesus was sending out his followers, some time after their first mission, on a longer journey, equipped and armed. Jesus expected most of them to possess swords already; any who did not must sell even those articles that they would most need for their journey, and buy one.

Others have tried to find evidence in this passage for a Zealot Jesus, but without the re-working that Eisler saw to be necess-

ary. Brandon says that 'the fact that some at least of the disciples
were accustomed to go about with concealed weapons, after
the manner of the Sicarii, is attested by Luke 22.38. The fact
that Jesus had to make sure that the disciples were armed on
this occasion indicates that their weapons were concealed in
their garments in Sicarii-fashion.'[16] Brandon, having assumed
that vv. 35–38 mean that Jesus made sure his disciples were
armed before going to the garden, naturally finds Luke's story
unconvincing. 'Luke', he says, 'endeavours to reduce' the significance of the arming 'by saying that Jesus did so in order to
fulfil a prophecy, and that he considered two swords enough
for this purpose. The ascription of such an artificial fulfilment
of an obscure passage of Isaiah to Jesus on such an occasion
does no credit to Jesus and lowers our estimation of the sensibility of Luke. With how many swords the disciples were armed
is immaterial; it is scarcely likely that it was only two.'[17]

The plain fact, on the contrary, would seem to be that any
attempt to interpret v. 38 literalistically as a source of factual
information renders it impossible to make sense of Luke's narrative as a whole. As Brandon suggests, we have to choose
between Luke's 'sensibility' on the one hand, and some kind of
reconstruction of the passage along literalistic lines, on the
other; we cannot have both, and for my part I prefer to choose
the former.

6

'The Testimony of Jesus is the Spirit of Prophecy'
(Revelation 19.10)

Ancient commentators on the Apocalypse, who are in any case rather few in number, rarely attempt to explain that perplexing verse, Rev. 19.10, which some modern exegetes have thought to be an interpolation. Those who do comment on it are sometimes concerned with anachronistic christological difficulties arising from the apparent identification of the glorified Christ with the angel who is a fellow-servant of the seer and his brethren (cf. Rev. 22.9, 13; 1.17), and they say little about the problem of ascertaining the meaning in this context of 'the testimony' or 'witness' (μαρτυρία) of Jesus and 'the Spirit of prophecy'. The three Greek commentators of the first millennium do, however, offer some suggestions. The earliest, Oecumenius of the sixth century, explains that the angel tells John that he is a fellow-servant of all those who testify that Christ is God incarnate, and 'all who testify to the lordship and deity of Christ are filled with the charisma of prophecy, and not I alone'.[1]

Oecumenius clearly understands 'the testimony of Jesus' to mean testimony about Jesus given by Christian believers, and 'the Spirit of prophecy' to be the inspiration of their witness to him. In view of the emphatic rejection of this exegesis by many later writers in favour of the view that μαρτυρία Ἰησοῦ should be interpreted subjectively as 'witness borne by Jesus', and that prophecy is inspired because it repeats and confirms Jesus' own personal testimony, the confidence with which Oecumenius offers this brief exposition is noteworthy, even though he is obviously mistaken in supposing that the Apocalyptist was concerned with the witness of Christians to christological orthodoxy.

Andrew of Caesarea is less confident. He presents two possible interpretations of ἡ μαρτυρία Ἰησοῦ. One is given in the following paraphrase: ' "Do not worship me," says the divine angel, "because I am foretelling the things that are to come; for confession of Christ or witness to him (ἡ γὰρ εἰς Χριστὸν ὁμολογία ἤγουν μαρτυρία) is that which provides the prophetic Spirit (αὕτη χορηγός ἐστι προφητικοῦ Πνεύματος)." '[2] Andrew's alternative suggestion is that the genitive is subjective; the meaning then is that the purpose of prophecy is to confirm Christ's own witness and to testify to Christian faith through the saints. His later successor at Caesarea, Arethas (probably ninth century), repeats Andrew's former interpretation and adds that the prophetic charisma is bestowed as a reward for witness borne for Christ, being itself similar to that witness: 'for prophecy was granted for the sake of my fellow-servants, the martyrs.'[3] Here, again, the testimony is witness *to* Jesus, and Arethas, despite the fact that he seems to regard the gift of prophecy as a reward for testifying rather than as the inspiration that enables a Christian to testify, shows a better appreciation of the nature of that witness, for he realizes that in the Apocalypse prophetic witness is directly related not to the profession of credal orthodoxy, but to testimony given under persecution and so to martyrdom.

Among the rather more numerous Latin commentators, Primasius is exceptional in taking notice of this passage. Like Oecumenius, Arethas, and Andrew in his former alternative, Primasius understands 'the testimony of Jesus' to mean 'witness borne to Jesus': not, however, by contemporary Christian prophets, as John certainly intended, but by the Spirit and the prophets in the scriptures, the witnesses signified by the presence of Moses and Elijah at the transfiguration and explicitly referred to by Jesus in the saying recorded at Luke 24.44.[4] These ancient commentators, then, see no difficulty in translating μαρτυρία Ἰησοῦ in this context as 'witness borne to Jesus', and, however fanciful may be their notions of the kind of testimony for which the prophetic gift is bestowed, in equating this witness with Spirit-inspired prophecy.

Modern exegetes, on the other hand, are more divided. In recent times many have favoured the second interpretation offered by Andrew of Caesarea. They understand the text to mean that the Spirit of prophecy re-presents in the contemporary church the witness borne by him who is the 'faithful witness' of Rev. 1.5. The witness of Jesus is identified by many with that 'good confession' (καλὴ ὁμολογία) which, according to I Tim. 6.13, he witnessed (μαρτυρήσαντος) before (ἐπί) Pontius Pilate. In the light of the very close connection so often and so strongly emphasized by New Testament writers between prophetic inspiration and witness to, or confession of (ὁμολογία), Jesus in circumstances of persecution such as are envisaged in the Apocalypse, and hence also between Spirit-inspired testimony and the nascent concept of Christian martyrdom, there may well be more merit than is often allowed in the exegesis of Rev. 19.10 which interprets Ἰησοῦ as an objective genitive and identifies the operation of the Spirit of prophecy with the confession of Jesus made in times of persecution under pressure to deny him. Examination of this question also involves some consideration of I. Tim. 6.12f. It ought properly to form part of a much wider study of the concept of 'witness' in the New Testament as a whole. Much work, however, has been recently done on this subject,[5] and such a study extends far beyond the scope of the present essay.

H. B. Swete tried to combine the subjective and objective interpretations of μαρτυρία Ἰησοῦ: 'While the original sense (i.e., subjective, as in 1.2) is never wholly out of sight, the latter (i.e., objective) probably predominates here.' According to Swete the passage means that 'the possession of the prophetic Spirit, which makes a true prophet, shows itself in a life of witness to Jesus which perpetuates His witness to the Father and to Himself'.[6] Many other exegetes have come down more firmly on the side of the subjective sense. I. T. Beckwith comments laconically: 'The testimony of Jesus: i.e. the truth revealed by Jesus. . . . The Spirit of Jesus is testifying in the prophet.'[7] Similarly M. Kiddle: 'The testimony borne by Jesus is the breath of all prophecy. The prophet . . . proclaims the mind of Christ.'[8] This Pauline concept is again evoked by R. H. Preston and A. T. Hanson: 'Jesus and his revelation of God, which Paul calls "the mind of Christ", is the content of the prophet's message, as it is of what John has been told to write in his book.'[9] For T. S. Kepler, the testimony of Jesus means 'the truth which Jesus' words and life reveal; God has divinely inspired Jesus with truth, as He also did the prophets of former times, to become the instrument or the incarnation of His message to mankind.'[10] A. M. Farrer links 'the testimony of Jesus' with the description of Jesus as 'the faithful witness' (Rev. 1.5; 3.14), to which he detects an allusion in the verse which immediately follows this passage: the rider on the white horse is 'called faithful and true'. To 'hold the witness of Jesus' means that 'men stand by his testimony, and confirm his passion with their martyrdom (12.11)'.[11] The angel, then, is telling John that 'it is not *my* testimony, but Christ's, that is the spirit of prophecy', and to worship Christ is not to direct worship away from God.

A very similar line to Farrer's is taken by G. B. Caird, who explains that 'to hold the testimony of Jesus is to stand by the principle which governed his incarnate life, to confirm and publish the testimony of his crucifixion with the testimony of martyrdom. . . . It is unthinkable that John . . . should have committed himself to the view that the sole source of his inspiration was his own testimony to Jesus, that he was in fact self-inspired. The testimony of Jesus is the spirit that inspires the prophets. It is the word spoken by God and attested by Jesus that the Spirit takes and puts into the mouth of Christian prophets.'[12] L. Morris, while keeping both options open, also favours the subjective interpretation,[13] as does H. Kraft, for whom this verse denotes the prophet's recognition that Jesus bestows his Spirit on him; it is the Spirit of Jesus who speaks.[14] A. A. Trites also is in no doubt that the testimony is that which was borne by Jesus, who is the 'faithful witness' in his death and hence also 'the firstborn from the dead' (1.5).[15]

None of these numerous attempts to explain ἡ μαρτυρία Ἰησοῦ on the basis of taking Ἰησοῦ as a subjective genitive seems, however, to give a satisfactory interpretation in this context, that is to say, in this part of the Apocalypse. The great vision has reached its climax; and the central theme of the vision is the struggle to the death, and beyond death, between the spiritual powers represented by faithful witness to Jesus and, on the other side, the worship of the Beast. In this lurid scene of persecution, agony, death, the destruction of 'Babylon' and the triumphant marriage-feast of the Lamb, the pietistic and moralizing generalities offered by some of these commentators are strangely out of place. The angel is not talking, as Swete supposed, about a *life* of witness to Jesus, but about the crisis of persecution: the choice between confessing Christ in the face of death or apostatizing: not about a general 'witness' of Jesus 'to the Father and to Himself', but about Jesus as the prototype of faithful martyrs like Antipas at Pergamum (2.13). Nor is the angel making, as Kiddle would have it, a general observation that prophets proclaim the mind of Christ. As the angel is speaking, the last battle is about to begin, and the Beast and his false prophet are about to be cast alive into a lake of fire. It would scarcely be a time for him to offer the theological comment, however true in itself, that the Spirit communicates through prophets 'the truth revealed in Jesus'.

What, after all, *is* 'the testimony borne by Jesus'? Most of the interpretations that have been offered of this are extremely vague, on the lines of Kepler's 'the truth which Jesus' words and life reveal', and to try to elucidate it by reference to the Pauline 'mind of Christ' is only to misinterpret the latter phrase and so to render the former still more obscure. Farrer and Caird suggest a meaning for 'Jesus' testimony' which is both less vague and more relevant to the context. According to them it is identical with 'his passion'; it is 'the testimony of his crucifixion'. Yet if the witness of Jesus is his actual death it might indeed be possible to say that his witness (that is, the crucifixion) inspires Christian martyrs to die, but scarcely that it is the inspiration of *prophecy*. Martyrs and prophets, it is true, are very closely related, but martyrdom is not itself a form of prophecy. The 'Spirit of prophecy' can only be the inspiration of prophetic utterance.

What utterance of Jesus, then, could this 'testimony' be? If it is an inspiration for Christian prophets resisting the pressure to worship the Beast, it must be a testimony borne by Jesus in a similar situation of persecution, that is, at his trial. The synoptic tradition contains an affirmative answer of Jesus to the high priest's question whether he is the Messiah (Mark 14.62, following the most probable reading): 'I am, and you will see the Son of man sitting at the right hand of the Power and coming with the clouds of heaven.' According to Matthew's version (26.64), Jesus replies with the ambiguous 'It is you who said this', and his answer in the Lucan narrative is also ambiguous: 'If I tell you, you will not believe; and if I ask, you will not answer'; and to a second question, 'Are you then the Son of God?', his reply is 'You say that I am' (Luke 22.67–70). The question whether a man held the basic Christian belief that Jesus is the Christ, the Son of God, was one which certainly would have to be either affirmed or denied before persecutors; but it could not possibly be answered by repeating the words of Jesus. If they represent his 'testimony', this could not become the inspiration of the prophet-confessors. Nor is the synoptic record of the answer of Jesus to Pilate any less meagre: 'You say (that I am king of the Jews)' (Mark 15.2; Matt. 27.11; Luke 23.3). It is not any utterance, but rather the silence of Jesus before Pilate, which is emphasized in the synoptic gospels.

A different tradition, however, may lie behind I Tim. 6.13, which appears to mean that Jesus bore witness in the form of the good confession (ὁμολογία) before Pilate. Commentators have often sought to bring this passage into line with the early baptismal creeds, supposing Timothy's own ὁμολογία, which is set in parallel with that of Jesus, to be his baptismal profession of faith. Pilate is, indeed, mentioned in summary expositions of the gospel, such as Acts 3.13; 4.27; 13.28, and in early credal formulas such as Ignatius, *Trallians* 9.1; *Smyrnaeans* 1.2, and Justin's *First Apology* 13.3 and 61.13. If this passage is to be reckoned among such references to Pilate as these, ἐπί would then mean 'in the time of'. C. H. Turner argues that a confession of Jesus before Pilate appears only in the Fourth Gospel, which is unlikely to have been known to the author of I Timothy, and he interprets the ὁμολογία of Jesus as his actual death,[16] being followed in this respect by J. Jeremias,[17] J. N. D. Kelly,[18] H. von Campenhausen[19] and M. Dibelius.[20] This interpretation was anticipated by Theodoret,[21] who paraphrases the text thus: καλὴν δὲ ὁμολογίαν τοῦ Κυρίου τὴν τῆς οἰκουμένης κέκληκε σωτηρίαν. ὑπερ αὐτῆς γὰρ τὸπάθος ὑπέμεινεν. It is, however, most improbable. μαρτυρεῖν, used absolutely, passes over from the sense of 'to witness' to that of 'to be a martyr' in the *Martyrdom of Polycarp* (1.1; 19.1; 21.1), Hegesippus[22] and Irenaeus (*Adv. haer.* III, 3.4), and is perhaps beginning to approach this meaning in I *Clement* 5.3–7; but there seems to be no parallel to the conjunction of μαρτυρεῖν in this latter sense with ὁμολογία. For ὁμολογία, though a technical term for a martyr's confession before his judges,[23] and therefore very closely associated with the death which, as Justin said,[24] was the appointed penalty for confession, never actually means 'martyrdom' in the sense of a martyr's death. Indeed, by the time of the persecution at Lyons and Vienne in 177 the distinction was beginning to be drawn between the μάρτυς whom Christ deemed worthy to be 'taken up' in the course of his ὁμολογία, and who thus sealed it with his death, and the ὁμολογητής who survived as a 'confessor' but not as a 'martyr'.[25] Nor is it likely that in I Tim. 6.13 means 'in the time of'. Pilate is mentioned in the speeches of Acts and in early credal statements with different aims in view. In Acts 4.27 it is to prove the necessity of the death of the Messiah from Psalm 2.2. In Acts. 3.13; 13.28, it is to emphasize that the Roman authority exculpated Jesus. In Ignatius and later credal formulations reference to the death of Jesus 'in the time of Pontius Pilate' is intended to anchor the gospel events in secular history. The present reference to Pilate seems to locate Jesus' 'good confession'. He witnessed it in Pilate's presence, like a Christian confessor before his judge; and the allusion must be either to the answer to Pilate recorded by the synoptists, as Baldensperger[26] and Windisch[27] believe (the former remarking that Jesus replied affirmatively to Pilate's question on his messiahship while otherwise remaining silent), or to a tradition, perhaps lying behind the Fourth Gospel, of a more extended dialogue between Jesus and Pilate. It is perhaps just conceivable that the author of the Pastoral Epistles knew the Fourth Gospel itself and its account of how Jesus witnessed to the truth before Pilate.

In any case, it is difficult to see how this ὁμολογία of Jesus could be identified with the Spirit of prophecy which inspires confessors. For John Jesus is, indeed, the μάρτυς ὁ πιστός, but the parallel with Antipas, Christ's faithful witness who was killed at Pergamum (Rev. 2.13), suggests that μάρτυς should here be understood in the sense of 'martyr', as it is in the *Epistle of Lyons and Vienne*.[28] In fact, μάρτυς, applied also to the martyr-prophets of Rev. 11.3 and to the saints of Rev. 17.6, slain by the persecuting power of 'Babylon', has already taken on the sense of 'martyr' in the Apocalypse. Jesus is the archetypal martyr, but the prophetic Spirit is surely inspiring confessors to bear their testimony to him, not to repeat such testimony as he was believed to have uttered at his trial.

This objective sense also suits the usage of the expression μαρτυρία Ἰησοῦ elsewhere in the Apocalypse. John bore witness to the gospel ('the word of God') and to the Christian profession of belief about ('testimony to') Jesus (1.2), and for this, i.e., for his faithful testimony, he was exiled to Patmos (1.9). It was for the word of God as the testimony which they held that the martyrs were slaughtered (6.9). This is the μαρτυρία which the two prophets (11.7) completed before their death, and the 'word of testimony' (i.e., confession of Christ before persecutors) by which the loyal martyrs overcame the Accuser (12.11). Faithful Christians keep God's commandments and maintain their witness to Jesus (12.17); and at 20.4 we see the triumph of the souls of those who had been beheaded for testifying to Jesus and proclaiming the word or gospel of God. ἔχειν μαρτυρίαν (6.9; 12.17; 19.10) appears to mean: 'to maintain' or 'to hold fast to' the confessors' testimony; it is thus parallel to the idea of 'keeping my word and not denying my name' (3.8); It is a quite different concept from that of the inward testimony (μαρτυρία) of God concerning his Son, which the believer, according to I John 5.9f., possesses (ἔχει) in himself through the indwelling of the Spirit.

The objective interpretation of μαρτυρία Ἰησοῦ was favoured by R. H. Charles,[29] who, however, supposed that 19.9b–10 might be an interpolation, partly because testimony to Jesus is here restricted to prophets, whereas at 22.9 the prophets of whom the angel is the fellow-servant are all those who 'keep the words of this book'; but the distinction is unreal: 'those who maintain testimony to Jesus' and are inspired to do so by the Spirit of prophecy (19.10) are not a special 'order' of prophets, but, ideally, include all Christian people. Lohmeyer[30] seems to take the genitive case in the same sense, although he does not make this entirely clear. He makes another unnecessary distinction between the martyrs who *have* the testimony and, on the other hand, ordinary believers who witness. Glasson[31] gives the sense of the passage as follows: 'Those who bear testimony to Jesus are inspired like the prophets. Angels and prophets were alike concerned with testimony to Jesus. They did not draw attention to themselves, and so any kind of honour or worship (such as John had offered to the angel) was inappropriate.' This is surely right, with the proviso that these prophets are not the scriptural prophets, but the contemporary confessors, including John himself. As Féret[32] expresses it, testimony is rendered by the seer to Jesus under the inspiration of the Spirit of prophecy.

John's phrase, μαρτυρία Ἰησοῦ, is thus a parallel expression to the μαρτύριον τοῦ Κυρίου ἡμῶν of II Tim. 1.8, and closely resembles the Pauline use of μαρτύριον when it is virtually synonymous with εὐαγγέλιον,[33] and Polycarp's allusion to the μαρτύριον τοῦ σταυροῦ (*Ep.* 7.1). But John is speaking of testimony of a special kind: the witness of the martyr-confessor. The synoptic tradition has much to say about this; for it carries Christ's promise of plenary inspiration. The prediction in the synoptic apocalypse that his followers will suffer persecution is accompanied by the promise that they need not be anxious beforehand about what they are to say in court, for 'whatever will be given you in that hour, that you are to speak; for it is not you who speak, but the Holy Spirit' (Mark 13.11), or, in Matthew's version, 'but the Spirit of your Father that speaks in you' (Matt. 10.19f.; cf. Luke 12.11f.). A second parallel in Luke to this promise is: 'I will give you a mouth and wisdom which all your opponents will not be able to withstand or refute' (21.15). Trial before governors and kings is the disciple's opportunity to testify: ἀποβήσεται ὑμῖν εἰς μαρτύριον (Luke 21.13); εἰς μαρτύριον αὐτοῖς καὶ τοῖς ἔθνεσιν (Matt. 10.18). The faithful witness who acknowledges Jesus before men will himself be acknowledged before the heavenly court of God's angels (Luke 12.8) or 'before my Father in heaven' (Matt. 10.32). In these assurances there lies the root of the Christian concept of martyrdom and the source of its strength.

The obverse side of the promise of inspiration for loyal confession is warning against denial. ὁμολογεῖν and ἀρνεῖσθαι are the alternative possibilities for the Christian in times of persecution (Matt. 10.32f.; Luke 12.9), and such passages as Rev. 2.13 and 3.8 and Hermas, *Sim.* IX,28.4 reveal the anxiety of the church's leaders lest their followers should 'deny'. Hence the prominence of warnings against 'being ashamed' of Christ and his words, as in Mark 8.38, or of 'the testimony of the Lord' in II Tim. 1.8, or 'denying' him, as in Matt. 10.33; Luke 12.9, and the 'saying' or hymn in II Tim. 2.12:

> If we endure, we shall also reign with him;
> if we deny him, he also will deny us.

Most impressive of all is Luke's identification of blasphemy against the Holy Spirit with the denial of Christ. In the context into which Luke transfers the saying about this blasphemy, it appears as the converse of confession; whereas the confessor will be taught by the Holy Spirit what to say at his trial, the apostate who rejects the inspiration of the Spirit commits the unforgivable sin (Luke 12.10–12).

The witnessing Christian is thus an inspired prophet. It is for witness to the end of the earth that the Spirit is given at Pentecost (Acts 1.8). According to John 15.26f., witness to Jesus is borne by the Spirit sent by Jesus from the Father to his disciples, the Spirit of truth to which Jesus himself had testified (John 18.37; cf. I John 5.6), and the Spirit's witness is also that of the disciples themselves. Indeed, persecuted disciples of Christ are

the successors of the prophets of the Old Testament: 'so persecuted they the prophets who were before you' (Matt. 5.12;
Luke 6.23). Stephen is presented in Acts 6–7 as the example of
the prophetic witness for whom the promise of inspiration has
been fulfilled. He is the ideal martyr-prophet,[34] for testimony
before persecutors naturally culminates in the death of the inspired witness. The background of this Christian concept of the
prophet-martyr is the tradition that prophets of the Old Testament had themselves been persecuted and put to death. This
is deeply rooted in many parts of the New Testament: in the
parable of the vineyard (Matt. 21.34–36), in the woes on the
Pharisees and scribes whose ancestors slew the prophets whose
tombs they now revere (Matt. 23.29–36; Luke 11.47–51), in the
lament of Jesus over Jerusalem (Matt. 23.37; Luke 13.34), at the
climax of Stephen's speech (Acts 7.52), in Paul's ferocious attack
on the Jews in I Thess. 2.15, in Heb. 11.37 and James 5.10, and
in the re-enactment of the killing of Old Testament prophetic
witnesses at Rev. 11.3. This tradition was established in Judaism, as is evidenced by Jubilees 1.12, the Martyrdom of Isaiah,
and numerous rabbinic allusions, and in the later *Vitae Prophetarum* all the prophets are also martyrs.

Throughout the New Testament the inspired witnesses to
Christ are engaged in a struggle against the opposition of false
prophets: Bar-Jesus (Acts 13.6–12), who tries, as a prophet of
recalcitrant Judaism, to prevent the conversion of a prominent
Gentile, the prophetess at Thyatira (Rev. 2.20), the false prophet
who serves the Beast (Rev. 16.13; 20.10) and, like the false
prophets predicted in the synoptic apocalypse (Mark 13.22;
Matt. 24.24), deludes the people with signs and wonders (Rev.
19.20). The problem of distinguishing the true prophet from the
false is as difficult in the church as in the Old Testament. The
criteria are 'their fruits' and, above all, whether or not they
testify to Christ; for this is the essential task of the Christian
prophet, and this is what the Spirit inspires him to do. Thus,
while a false prophet may curse Jesus, it is the mark of authentic
inspiration to proclaim 'Jesus is Lord' (I Cor. 12.3); only those
prophetic spirits, that is, inspired prophets, who confess that
Jesus is the Messiah who has come in the flesh are of God (I
John 4.1–3; II John 7).

There is more to be said than most commentators allow for
Baldensperger's view that Timothy is represented at I Tim. 6.12
as a confessor in a time of persecution. It is a theory which goes

back to Theodore of Mopsuestia: ' *"confessus es"*, *hoc est*, *"passus es"*.*'[35]* Timothy is said to have confessed (ὡμολόγησας) the good confession (καλὴν ὁμολογίαν) before many witnesses. Many exegetes, among them Turner, Kelly, von Campenhausen and Dibelius, interpret this as a reference to the baptismal profession of faith. ὁμολογίαν could certainly be appropriately used in that sense, as Rom. 10.9f. indicates, though in specifically religious contexts in the New Testament it appears most often with a reference to 'confession' as opposed to 'denial' under persecution, and to the corresponding acknowledgment by Christ of the confessors (Matt. 10.32; Luke 12.8; John 9.22; 12.42; Rev. 3.5). Käsemann[36] rightly rejects the baptismal reference on the ground of the parallel between the 'good confession' of Timothy and the 'good confession' of Christ, but he refers it to Timothy's ordination, which seems open to the same objection. This parallel between Christ's confession before Pilate and Timothy's confession in the presence of many witnesses (recalling the synoptic testimony 'before governors and kings' and 'to the Gentiles') strongly suggests that Timothy's confession was made in court. Whether this was an actual historical event, or whether a picture of 'Timothy' as an ideal church leader is being built up so as to include the presentation of him as a faithful witness in persecution is not relevant to this discussion. In either case the imprisonment of Timothy implied in Heb. 13.23 may well lie behind this passage.

This situation, then, where Jewish and Gentile opponents of Christianity are trying to make its adherents deny that Jesus is the Messiah, or to curse Christ (*Mart. Polyc.* 9.3), say that Caesar is Lord (ibid., 8.2), and swear by the τύχη of Caesar (ibid., 9.2), is the setting for the angel's assurance that it is the prophetic Spirit which inspires every confession of Jesus, and, conversely, that the form which inspired prophecy takes in this struggle is testimony to Jesus. This is the basis of the early church's 'pneumatology of martyrdom' which finds expression in the claim that the confessors of Lyons 'had the Holy Spirit as their counsellor' as they waited in prison,[37] in Tertullian's words to the martyrs, 'Grieve not the Spirit who has entered prison with you' (*Ad mart.* 1.3), and Cyprian's assertion that the confessor-bishop, although he ought not to surrender himself voluntarily, ought, when apprehended by the authorities, to speak, since 'God in us (*Deus in nobis positus*)' speaks in that hour.[38] Perhaps there is a difference of emphasis between this view of the martyr as Spirit-inspired, and therefore essentially a prophet-witness, and the 'christology of martyrdom' which develops side by side with it. According to the latter, it is Christ who suffers in the passion of the martyr;[39] Christ's death is re-presented in each martyrdom.[40] Then it is suffering and death for, with, and in Christ that is seen as the essence of martyrdom, rather than Spirit-inspired, prophetic, μαρτυρία Ἰησοῦ.

7

Martyrdom and Inspiration

The Christian Church owes its survival of almost three centuries of intermittent persecution during the critical period of its formation and growth, and its emergence at the end of that time as a movement powerful enough to establish a position of total dominance in the Roman Empire, to its clear and uncompromising idea of martyrdom. This was a tradition that it had inherited to a large extent from Judaism, like itself a martyr-religion in the sense of a religion that actively and systematically trained its adherents collectively (as distinct from the individual heroes produced by Graeco-Roman philosophies, such as Socrates, or the Stoic dissidents in the early empire) for a vocation to witness to their faith not only at the cost of, but actually by means of, suffering and death. For Christians, however, the conviction that the martyr was the ideal disciple held an even more central place in belief and practice, for it was rooted in the event that stood at the heart of the gospel, the death of Jesus. Their doctrine of martyrdom was, indeed, largely derived and developed out of the response of the orthodox Jewish resistance movement to the persecution under Antiochus Epiphanes, but there are significant differences of attitude between such writings as Daniel, II Maccabees and IV Maccabees, on the one hand, and the New Testament and second-century Christian literature on the other. The former tends to be primarily defensive. The stories told in Daniel and the accounts of the words and the heroic endurance of the Maccabean martyrs are designed to encourage their readers to resist the attempts of brutal heathen rulers to force them to abandon their religion – to worship idols, to eat unclean food, and so to apostatize from the Law. The Christian martyr, too, has to resist, through tor-

ture and death, the efforts of the authorities to make him re-
nounce his faith; but it is he who really takes the initiative. The
martyr is, as the word 'martyr' denotes, a witness, and as a
witness he is, as it were, on the offensive against the persecuting power. Unlike the Jewish martyr, his aim is not merely
passive resistance to attempts to compel him to abjure his ances-
tral way of life (as by forcing him to eat pork), but active testifying to a gospel. For the central point of conflict between the
church and both the synagogue and the Roman authorities lay
in the realm of belief. Their controversy turned on the cardinal
Christian belief that 'Jesus is Lord'. This was the essential theme
of the church's witness, provoking the Roman state in the second century to confront Christian believers with the demand
that they should curse Christ and acknowledge that 'Caesar is
Lord.'[1] The Christian was essentially a missionary, and martyrdom was for him the supreme and most effective mode of
evangelism. A trial of Christians before a Roman governor was
therefore always for them a show trial. It was their great opportunity for propaganda, when they could confess Christ before the rulers of the world. Death by a public execution set the
seal on their testimony in the presence of the crowds, and by
writing and circulating their *acta* the church secured for it still
wider and more lasting publicity.

This immensely significant idea could be expressed in a variety of theological terms and imagery. There was what might
be called a 'pneumatology' of martyrdom, in so far as the martyr's testimony was believed to be inspired by the Holy Spirit
and the Christian who confessed his faith in circumstances of
persecution was regarded as closely akin to the prophet as a
recipient of revelation and a proclaimer of God's word. It is this
aspect of the idea of martyrdom that it is the purpose of this
essay to explore. There was also a 'christology' of martyrdom,
a 'soteriology', an 'anthropology' and a 'demonology'.

All these facets of the idea of martyrdom have their roots in
the New Testament or in pre-Christian Judaism, and they find
parallel expression in such classical expositions of the early
church's thoughts on this subject as the *Martyrdom of Polycarp*
and the *Epistle of the Churches of Lyons and Vienne* to the churches
of Asia, describing the great outbreak of persecution in the year
177. By a 'christology' of martyrdom I mean the interpretation
of the faithful disciple's suffering and death as the imitation of
Christ, a concrete and literal realization of that death and burial

with Christ which is figuratively enacted in every convert's baptism (Rom. 6.3; Col. 2.12), and as the consummation of so intimate a personal union with Christ that the Lord himself can be said to suffer in the person of his loyal follower. In the New Testament this understanding finds expression in such passages as Acts 9.5 (to persecute the Christian community is to persecute Jesus himself); John 15.20 (Christ's disciples must expect to suffer similar persecution to that which was directed against their Master); the hymn quoted at II Timothy 2.11 ('If we have died with him, we shall also live with him; if we endure, we shall also reign with him'); and especially in I Peter, where it is very prominent, particularly in 4.13 ('Rejoice in so far as you share Christ's sufferings, that you may also rejoice and be glad when his glory is revealed'). It underlies the evident concern of Luke to draw a close parallel between the death of Jesus and that of Stephen, the first martyr. Ignatius, who does not use the actual 'martyr' terminology, dwells on this aspect of his approaching death: it is his entry upon true discipleship, it means the attainment of Christ, and by it he will become 'an imitator of my God'.[2] In the *Martyrdom of Polycarp* the theme of *imitatio Christi* is further developed in the correspondence between the details of his story and those of the Passion narratives in the gospels (1.2; 7.1), in the claim that the martyr becomes a participant in Christ (6.2), and in the writer's comment that, although the church's enemies were foolish to suppose that the surviving Christians might apostatize from Christ to worship the martyrs, they do love and reverence them as disciples and imitators of the Lord (17.3). Here, too, we find the belief that the Lord in person stands by the Christian sufferers and converses with them (2.2).

When martyrdom is interpreted in this christocentric fashion it is the actual suffering and death of the Christian disciple that is of primary significance rather than his verbal testimony; for, according to the *Epistle of Lyons and Vienne*, Christ himself suffers in the body of the martyr and defeats the devil there. In the same document the martyr Blandina is said to put on Christ, the invincible athlete, and, in the manner of her death, to be a representation of Christ on the cross.[3] It is probably under the influence of this emphasis on Christian martyrdom as participation in the suffering and death of Jesus that the word μάρτυς and its cognates tend in the second century to lose the sense of 'witness', at least as their primary meaning, and for a distinction to be drawn between the martyr who literally dies with Christ and the confessor who witnesses to him before persecutors but does not actually suffer the death penalty. Thus Tertullian, instead of using a Latin equivalent for μάρτυς in the sense of 'witness', has to take over the Greek word and employ it in Latin as a technical term for 'martyr', a person who has died for and with Christ.

The 'soteriology' of martyrdom takes up the idea that was so prominent in Judaism, that the death of the martyr effects atonement for Israel by expiating the people's sins or propitiating the wrath of God. The martyr's death, according to IV Maccabees (6.28f.; cf. 1.11; 17.22), makes satisfaction on behalf of the people, and his soul is a ransom for their souls. This is an interpretation of martyrdom that, although it seems to have been of cardinal importance for early Christian reflection on the significance of the death of Christ himself (cf. esp. Mark 10.45; Matt. 20.28), received comparatively little emphasis in respect of the sufferings of his disciples. Its influence, however, can probably be seen in the application of sacrificial imagery to martyrdom. Thus Paul speaks of the possibility that he may 'be poured as a libation upon the sacrificial offering' of the faith of the Christian community (Phil. 2.17; cf. II Tim. 4.6), Ignatius of his life as an exchange for his readers' lives (*Eph.* 21.1), and the *Martyrdom of Polycarp* (14.1f.) describes Polycarp as a 'whole burnt offering' and 'a rich and acceptable sacrifice'.

An 'anthropology' of martyrdom means, to use a rough and ready and perhaps rather unfair designation, a somewhat anthropocentric view, which treats the conflict waged by the martyr against his oppressors' efforts to make him recant as an external projection of the inward struggle in the human soul between the flesh and the spirit (in the sense of the lower nature or passions, on the one side, and the higher, rational, self on the other). This is a central theme of IV Maccabees, where the martyrs' heroic resistance to every form of torture, and their steadfast refusal to yield to any persuasion to abandon their loyalty to the Law, are a supreme example of the conquest of the passions by reason (λογισμός). The martyr, Eleazar, was 'king over the passions' (IV Macc. 7.10). It may be a little unfair to characterize this interpretation as anthropocentric, for it is of course assumed that the Maccabean loyalists are divinely inspired and fortified, and this presupposition underlies the author's description of Eleazar raising his eyes to heaven (which signifies communion with God) while he 'keeps his reason in-flexible' (IV Macc. 6.5f.). It is, nevertheless, an interpretation in which divine inspiration and personal communion with God are emphasized less strongly than the classical cardinal virtues, especially fortitude and self-control under the hegemony of reason. It thus has close links with Stoic morality and furnishes a bridge between Christian ideas of martyrdom and the philo-sophical tradition of heroic virtue. Thus Clement of Alexandria refers to the work of Timotheus of Pergamum on the fortitude of the philosophers,[4] and Tertullian commends the example of pagan 'martyrs' such as Mucius Scaevola, Heraclitus, Empe-docles and Dido.[5] There may be a hint of a similar idea of transcendent heroism and of the conquest of the flesh by the spirit in the *Martyrdom of Polycarp* 2.3 (notwithstanding the wri-ter's insistence on 'the grace of Christ') where we are told that the martyrs despised worldly tortures, and that for them the fire was cool, because they were no longer human beings but already angels. It is a way of looking at martyrdom that soon lent itself to spiritualization: the martyr is one particular kind of ascetic, and his example can be followed, even when there is no external persecution, by those who steadfastly practise ἀπάθεια.[6]

The 'demonology' of martyrdom is the reverse side, as it were, of the belief that the faithful confessor is inspired by the Holy Spirit and dies as an imitator of Christ and a participant in his victory over the demonic powers. Just as the real object of the persecutors' attack is not primarily their individual vic-tims but the faith that they profess and, ultimately, the God in whom they trust, so the opponent against whom the Christian 'athletes' contend is really the devil. Satan is the tempter of the faithful, seeking to cajole or frighten them into apostasy, pos-sessing Judas the archetypal traitor (Luke 22.3; John 13.27), trying to 'sift' the disciples of Jesus in the moment of the crisis of his arrest (Luke 22.31), sitting enthroned at a centre of the imperial cult where Christians were faced with the choice be-tween confession and denial (Rev. 2.13), and always, until his final overthrow, the present and active enemy (Rev. 12.9; 20.2). In the *Martyrdom of Perpetua* 10 the struggle is symbolized for Perpetua by her fight in a dream against an Egyptian wrestler, and it is Satan who 'eagerly strives' to make the martyrs of Lyons and Vienne utter some blasphemy, who supposes that he has 'devoured' (cf. I Peter 5.8) Biblis who had 'denied' instead of confessing Christ, and who inspires the persecutors who are 'full of the devil' and are his ministers.[7]

It is, however, with the positive aspect that we are now concerned: the confessor of Christ as a Spirit-possessed and prophet-like person. According to this tradition, it is the faithful Christian's testimony that is of central significance. To deliver it may well mean to incur death, but whether the result is death, a lesser penalty such as imprisonment or exile, or, exceptionally, release is comparatively unimportant. Death is almost incidental; it is the witness before hostile authorities that is the essence of 'martyrdom' and the role of the Spirit is not primarily to bring consolation and strength in physical suffering, but to inspire confessors to proclaim the lordship of Christ with uninhibited freedom (παρρησία). This concept, in which the inspiration of the Spirit finds expression in evangelistic witness, has deep roots in the Old Testament. It is linked with the vocation of the whole people of God: ' "You are my witnesses," says the Lord, "and my servant whom I have chosen, that you may know and believe me and understand that I am He" ' (Isa. 43.10); and to the 'servant . . . in whom my soul delights', who is either identical with, or symbolical of, God's faithful witnessing people, it is said: 'I have put my Spirit upon him' (Isa. 42.1). Within this general vocation to witness there is the special and more sharply focused testimony of faithful individuals, more particularly in the face of hostility and persecution. It is probably in these circumstances that the devotee of the Law prays in Psalm 119.41–46 for inspiration to testify to it before rulers:

> Let thy steadfast love come to me, O Lord,
> . . . then shall I have an answer for those who taunt me,
>   for I trust in thy word.
> And take not the word of truth utterly out of my mouth . . .
> I will also speak of thy testimonies before kings,
>   and shall not be put to shame.

In the unprecedented situation of religious persecution in the Maccabean era the 'wise', typified by the figure of Daniel himself and the 'Three Children', are confessors and sufferers for Judaism (Dan. 12.2f.), and, as with the righteous man, the 'son of God' and 'servant of the Lord', of Wisdom 2.12ff., faithful witness carries the assurance of resurrection or immortality (Wisdom 3.1–8).

The prophets come to be regarded not only as men inspired

by God's Spirit but also as martyrs. Collectively, the prophets were messengers of God to Israel whose message was constantly rejected: 'The Lord,' says the Chronicler, 'sent persistently to them by his messengers . . . but they kept mocking the messengers of God, despising his words, and scoffing at his prophets' (II Chron. 36.15f.). They were even put to death: 'I will send witnesses to them, that I may witness against them, but they will not hear, and will slay the witnesses also' (Jubilees 1.12). Witness and prophecy are thus identified, and the prophet gives his testimony under the inspiration of the Spirit. Thus we read in II Chronicles 24.20f.:

> The Spirit of God took possession of Zechariah the son of Jehoiada the priest; and he stood above the people, and said to them, "Thus says God, 'Why do you transgress the commandments of the Lord, so that you cannot prosper? Because you have forsaken the Lord, he has forsaken you.' " But they conspired against him, and by command of the king they stoned him with stones in the court of the house of the Lord.

Later, Isaiah was reckoned as another Spirit-inspired prophet–martyr, who was absorbed in a vision of the Lord (like Stephen, according to Acts 7.55f.) so that he did not hear the order to recant, and whose 'lips spoke with the Holy Spirit' until he was sawn in twain (Martyrdom of Isaiah 5.7, 14).

Individually, each of the Hebrew prophets came to have martyrdom ascribed to him, and the stories of their trials and sufferings typified the ideal of the Jewish martyr. To such prophets as Zechariah and Jeremiah and Isaiah there were added Abel, Abraham, Isaac, Joseph, Phinehas and Daniel as examples of faithful servants of God who were ready to suffer for their loyalty, even though they did not necessarily have to undergo actual death (IV Macc. 6.17, 23; 13.9; 14.20; 16.3, 20f.; 18.1, 11f., 23). This tradition passes over into Christianity. It is implied in the parable of the Wicked Tenants of the Vineyard, where the servants sent by the owner are ill-treated and killed (Mark 12.1–5), and where the murder of his son comes as the climax of the succession of martyrdoms. It is more explicitly stated in Jesus' denunciation of the scribes and Pharisees as the sons of those who killed the prophets (Matt. 23.29–33; Luke 11.47f.), by Paul who, again, sees the death of Jesus as the climax of the long story of Jewish persecution of the prophets (I Thess. 2.15), by Luke in the speech of Stephen, where the inspiration of the prophet-martyrs is related specifically to their role as foretellers of the coming of the 'Righteous One' (Acts 7.52), and by the writer to the Hebrews, for whom the prophets are examples of endurance (11.32ff.). Ignatius similarly speaks of the persecution of the prophets, whose inspiration he ascribes, somewhat in the manner of I Peter 1.11, to the grace of *Christ* (*Magn.* 8.2).

The further implication of the references in the New Testament to the persecution of the ancient prophets is that the disciples of Jesus stand in the same succession of inspired and suffering witnesses. Matthew's Great Sermon is addressed to the disciples of Jesus. It is they who receive the blessing that belongs to those who are persecuted for righteousness' sake; they are to rejoice and be glad 'for your reward is great in heaven, for so men persecuted the prophets who were before you' (Matt. 5.10–12). Jesus himself, whose death in Jerusalem will follow the pattern of the persecution of the prophets (Luke 13.33f.), will send a new succession of prophets and wise men and scribes, or, as Luke has it, prophets and apostles,

> some of whom you will kill and crucify, and some you will scourge in your synagogues and persecute from town to town, that upon you may come all the righteous blood shed on earth, from the blood of innocent Abel to the blood of Zechariah [Matthew adds 'the son of Barachiah'], whom you murdered between the sanctuary and the altar (Matt. 23.34f.; Luke 11.49f.).

For Paul, similarly, the persecution of the prophets was part of a single continuous story, which includes the death of Jesus and the expulsion of the apostle himself, and also the obstruction of his Gentile mission (I Thess. 2.15). Luke's account of the death of Stephen also implies very clearly that this martyrdom is to be understood against the background of the killing of the prophets and the murder of the Christ whom they had foretold (Acts 7.52–57). This inclusion of the disciples and missionary witnesses of Jesus within the succession of prophet–martyrs sets the keynote for the presentation of the Christian confessor in the New Testament writings as a person inspired and possessed by the Spirit in a special degree. Before we leave the allusion to the persecution of the Old Testament saints in Matthew 23.35, however, it may be worth noticing the strange reference to Zechariah as 'son of Barachiah'. It has some relevance to the history of early Christian understandings of martyrdom because of the curious appearance of the name Zechariah (Zacharias) in the story of the martyrs of Lyons and

Vienne. One Vettius Epagathus came forward courageously and testified to the innocence of the Christians. He was arrested himself, and

> was asked this one question, if he too were a Christian. And having confessed (ὁμολογήσαντος) in a very clear voice, he also was taken up into the inheritance (κλῆρος) of the martyrs, being called the advocate (παράκλητος) of Christians, but having within himself the Paraclete, the Spirit of Zacharias [a variant reading has 'the Spirit more than that of Zacharias'], which he showed through the fullness of love, being well pleased to lay down even his own life for the defence of the brethren.[8]

This passage of the *Epistle of Lyons and Vienne* is highly instructive as an illustration of the 'pneumatology of martyrdom'. The allusion to the 'Spirit of Zacharias', however, if that is the correct reading, as seems probable, appears to be unique. The *Epistle* offers a partial explanation: that Vettius was likened to the Lucan Zacharias because he 'walked in all the commandments and ordinances of the Lord, blameless' (Luke 1.6). This, however, suggests no real reason why the Paraclete, the inspirer of the martyr's confession, 'I am a Christian', should be called, or even compared with, the 'Spirit of Zacharias'. It is of course true that Zacharias, like the other chief characters in Luke's infancy stories, was an inspired prophet; he was 'filled with the Holy Spirit and prophesied' in the words of the *Benedictus* (Luke 1.67). This again, however, has no apparent connection with a martyr's inspired confession. There is the further complication that the name Zacharias stands second in the list of the martyrs of Lyons, in the Hieronymian martyrology and the martyrology of Bede after that of the bishop, Pothinus, and in Gregory of Tours and the Brussels MS 207–208 after that of Vettius Epagathus, which heads the list.[9] The suggestion is probably correct that this 'Zacharias' is not another martyr unmentioned in the *Epistle*, but a Christian surname given to Vettius on the lines of Ignatius' surname Theophorus.

The strong likelihood is that von Campenhausen is right in inferring that by 177 the Lucan Zacharias was already thought to have been an inspired martyr.[10] There was great confusion in antiquity between the various Zechariahs in the Bible. Zechariah the son of Jehoiada was, as we have seen, prominent in the tradition concerning martyr-prophets, and he continued to have an important place in rabbinic thought.[11] Sozomen's *Ecclesiastical History* concludes with the discovery of his remains at Caphar-Zechariah near Eleutheropolis in Palestine. A local landlord was told by the prophet in a dream to dig in a garden, where he would find a double casket, wooden within, leaden without, together with a crystal vessel of water and two snakes 'of moderate size, gentle and harmless so as to appear quite tame'. The prophet was duly found, dressed in a white robe 'as being, I suppose', says Sozomen, showing some confusion with Zechariah's father, 'a priest'. Beneath his feet, outside the coffin, there lay a child who had been given a royal burial, with a golden crown, golden sandals, and rich vesture. The abbot of the monastery at Gerar, another Zacharias, came across an old and uncanonical Hebrew document, which showed that on the seventh day after Zechariah's martyrdom the son of King Joash died suddenly, and the king buried him at the prophet's feet by way of expiation. Sozomen adds that the prophet was intact, with his hair shorn, a straight nose, a beard of moderate length, a rather short head, and eyes somewhat deeply set and over-shadowed by the eyebrows.[12] The *Vitae Prophetarum* included among the *spuria* of Epiphanius tell us that the priests buried Zechariah beside his father, and that from then onwards there were no revelations in the Temple, by theophanies, visions of angels, oracles, ephod, or Urim and Thummim.

Yet although Zechariah the son of Jehoiada was famous as the prototype of inspired prophet–martyrs and attracted to himself some interesting legends, he had early become confused with the prophet Zechariah the son of Barachiah, as our text in Matthew shows. This caused much trouble to ancient commentators. Chrysostom, for instance, asks who the Zechariah of Matthew 23.35 can be: some say it is the father of John the Baptist, some the prophet Zechariah, some another person, a priest with two names whom scripture also calls Jehoiada.[14] Chrysostom does not attempt an answer to his own rather confused question (he has the excuse that in the LXX the son of Jehoiada appears as Azariah). Jerome does better. He explains that some say this is indeed the son of Barachiah, the eleventh of the Twelve Prophets, but that he is never said to have been killed between the temple and the altar; indeed, in that Zechariah's time there were only ruins of the temple. Some think Matthew is referring to the father of the Baptist, slain, according to apocryphal fancies, because he proclaimed the advent of Christ. Others think this is really the Zechariah who was killed by Joash; but he was the son of Jehoiada the priest, not of

Barachiah. Jerome adds that in the Gospel of the Nazarenes the text reads 'son of Jehoiada' for 'son of Barachiah', and that Christians of the simpler sort point out certain red rocks between the ruins of the temple and the altar, or in the gateways leading to Siloam, which they believe to be stained with the blood of Zechariah.[15]

By the fourth century there was thus a well-established confusion between three Zechariahs. In fact the introduction of Luke's Zacharias into the conflation of the son of Barachiah with the son of Jehoiada was already known to Origen, and developed by him. According to Origen the reference in Matthew 23.35 is to the father of the Baptist. Scripture does not tell us that he was the son of Barachiah, nor that he was slain by the scribes and Pharisees between the temple and the altar; but there is a tradition that there was a place in the temple reserved for virgins to stand and pray. Mary went there after the birth of her child, and those who knew of the birth objected. Zacharias then defended her right to stand there as a virgin, and for this apparent breach of the Law he was slain between the temple and the altar. Origen makes the rather effective point that those who reject that story must explain why Jesus says that the scribes and Pharisees actually killed Zacharias themselves (ἐφονεύσατε), not that, as in the case of the prophets, they are the sons of those who so acted. He adds, however, that there may have been two men called Zacharias, and two fathers of men called Zacharias with the same name.[16] Elsewhere Origen adds another stone to this edifice of confusion: he claims that Josephus says that the Lucan Zacharias was the son of Barach, having identified the father of the Baptist with Josephus' Zechariah, son of Barach, murdered in the temple during the Jewish War.[17]

Another story to account for the supposed martyrdom of Luke's Zacharias is told by Epiphanius, perhaps from an early Gnostic source: Zacharias was killed in the temple because he had discovered that the object of Jewish worship was a man in the form of an ass.[18] A third tale, known to Peter of Alexandria,[19] and later appended to the *Protevangelium of James*, makes Zacharias the high priest (8.3). Herod's officers appear, hunting down the children, and ask the whereabouts of the child John, who has escaped with his mother into the country. Zacharias refuses to tell them, makes a martyr's confession in the curious form, 'I am a martyr of God', and is slain beside the altar (ibid., 23f.).

It would seem, then, that the process that led to the identification of the Paraclete that Vettius the martyr 'had within himself' with the 'Spirit of Zacharias' was as follows: Zacharias was known from Luke 1.67 to have been a Spirit-possessed prophet; he was identified with the Zacharias of Matthew 23.35 (who had already been confused with the canonical prophet, the son of Barachiah) and was therefore believed to have been a martyr; he may also have already been thought to have been not only a priest, as in the third gospel, but high priest, and it is therefore conceivable that he would be regarded as an inspired prophet on the ground of John 11.51, which ancient commentators generally took to mean that the high priest was endowed with the gift of prophecy *ex officio*.

All this, however, is of very minor importance in comparison with the main point, which is the fact that the *Epistle of Lyons and Vienne* provides such striking evidence of the early church's belief in the plenary inspiration of those who witnessed to Christ before persecutors. Since Vettius was spokesman or advocate for Christ and his disciples, it was really the Paraclete himself who spoke in him. His companions, says the *Epistle*, had the Holy Spirit as their counsellor (σύμβουλος).[20] Similarly Tertullian urges confessors not to 'grieve the Spirit who has entered prison with you' (*Ad mart.* 1.3), and Cyprian claims that it is the duty of a Christian leader to speak, if he is arrested and brought before the authorities, because the one who really speaks is 'God within us (*Deus in nobis positus*)'.[21] Here lay the great strength of the Christian movement; it was realistically understood that Christ's followers could expect only hatred and persecution, since that had been the lot of Christ himself; but in the decisive choice between confession and denial, and in witness before heathen rulers, it would be the invincible Spirit that would control and inspire their actions and words.

This belief was already firmly established by the time of the formation of the synoptic traditions. Certain passages in the gospels constitute the foundation of the development of the Christian idea of witness and martyrdom as a primary operation of the Holy Spirit. In the synoptic apocalypse (Mark 13.9–11 and the parallel at Luke 21.12–15) Jesus warns his disciples of coming persecution (this warning being also reproduced at Matt. 24.9ff.): 'They will deliver you up to councils (συνέδρια) and you will be beaten in synagogues; and you will stand before governors and kings for my sake, to bear testimony before them. And the gospel must first be preached to all nations.' An unambiguous promise of direct inspiration accompanies this warning: 'And when they bring you to trial and deliver you up, do not be anxious beforehand what you are to say; but say whatever is given you in that hour, for it is not you who speak, but the Holy Spirit.' According to Luke, Jesus, having warned the disciples that they will be brought before kings and governors, tells them that 'This will be a time for you to bear testimony.' Persecution is thus the great opportunity to further the Christian mission by public witness, which, being divinely inspired, must ultimately prove irresistible. 'Settle it therefore in your minds, not to meditate beforehand how to answer; for I will give you a mouth and wisdom, which none of your adversaries will be able to withstand or contradict.' Here the phrase 'a mouth and wisdom' is equivalent to prophetic inspiration, Jesus himself being the giver of it, as, according to Luke and John, he is the giver or mediator of the Holy Spirit.

The promise that Mark sets in the context of the eschatological discourse appears in Matthew (10.17–20) in the 'mission charge' at the sending out of the Twelve. Again, it reflects the conditions in which the post-resurrection witness of the church was being carried out. Luke reproduces the promise again in a remarkable context at 12.11f.: 'And when they bring you before the synagogues and the rulers and the authorities, do not be anxious how or what you are to answer or what you are to say; for the Holy Spirit will teach you in that very hour what you ought to say.' Luke's context is, first, as in the Matthaean 'mission charge', the eschatological promise: 'Every one who acknowledges me before men, the Son of man also will acknowledge before the angels of God; but he who denies me before men will be denied before the angels of God' (Luke 12.8f.; Matt. 10.32f.), the first part of which is closely paralleled in Mark 8.38// Luke 9.26. Here the scene in an earthly court where a faithful confessor 'acknowledges' (ὁμολογήσῃ) the Lord is projected on to the heavenly court. Just as the Christian disciple confesses Christ, so before the angels of the heavenly court Christ will testify to the faithfulness of his servant. So, too, the apostate who has taken the opposite course and denied (ὁ ἀρνήσαμενος) Christ will in turn be denied by him in the presence of the angels. In Luke the negative side of this combined promise and warning is developed by the insertion into this same context of the saying concerning blasphemy against the Holy Spirit (Luke

12.10; Mark 3.29; Matt. 12.32). The setting of this in Mark and Matthew is quite different, and Luke's introduction of it into the context of the promise that confessors can rely on plenary inspiration is very striking. 'Every one who speaks a word against the Son of man will be forgiven; but he who blasphemes against the Holy Spirit will not be forgiven.' Luke evidently understands the blasphemy that is unforgivable to be the denial of Christ before men, to which he has just referred. Such denial amounts to a direct repudiation of the promised inspiration of the Spirit. It is the blasphemy against the Spirit, interpreted by Luke as the Spirit operating in the missionary witness of the church, and transferred by him from the context of the Galilean mission of the earthly Jesus, in which Mark and Matthew place it, to that of the Christian confessor on trial before synagogues, rulers and authorities. This is the disastrous act of apostasy, which the missionary church treated in a manner similar to that in which an army treats desertion in face of the enemy. Luke apparently believes that it was possible to 'speak a word against the Son of man' during the earthly life of Jesus without incurring this ultimate sin; the Spirit-inspired community with its commission to witness to the end of the earth (Acts 1.8) had not yet come into being, and the unforgivable sin belongs to the post-resurrection, or rather for Luke the post-Pentecostal, era of mission.[22]

The promise of inspiration and its fulfilment in early Christian experience is a frequent theme in the New Testament writings. Acts 4.5ff. describes the first appearance of apostles before a court. A most formal and solemn assembly of rulers and elders and scribes, with the high priest and all who were of the high-priestly family, inquire by what power or by what name Peter and John had healed the crippled man at the temple gate and preached to the crowd. In reply Peter makes his apologia 'filled with the Holy Spirit', and the court has to recognize the characteristic mark of inspiration, boldness or freedom of speech (παρρησία). After their release the Christian community corporately prays that God may grant his servants to speak his word with all παρρησία, and in answer the place where they were praying was shaken, and 'they were all filled with the Holy Spirit and spoke the word of God with boldness' (Acts 4.29–31). Thus on their next appearance before the authorities Peter and the apostles were able to claim: 'We are witnesses to these things, and so is the Holy Spirit whom God has given to those who obey him' (Acts 5.32). The story of Stephen is so told as to leave no doubt that he is an inspired man. He is full of grace and power; his opponents cannot withstand the wisdom and the Spirit with which he speaks (Acts 6.8–10); when he begins his apologia before the sanhedrin the members of the court see that his face is like the face of an angel (Acts 6.15); and as his hearers turn on him in fury he, 'full of the Holy Spirit', sees the glory of God and Jesus standing at the right hand of God (Acts 7.55). Stephen is, in fact, presented by Luke as a prophet and seer and martyr.

Of the Pauline writings Philippians is the most important from this standpoint. Paul's imprisonment is a means by which the progress of the gospel is furthered; it brings him to the attention of the whole praetorium and to all others, and it encourages his Christian brethren to speak God's word fearlessly; through the gift of the Spirit of Jesus Christ he can confidently hope that he will not be put to shame (that is, fail to meet the challenge), but that Christ will be honoured in his person, whether he dies or survives, with all παρρησία; suffering for Christ's sake is a sign of perdition to the persecutors, but of salvation to the sufferers; he and his supporters are engaged in a contest together (like athletes) in the faith of the gospel (Phil. 1.12–14, 19f., 27–29). Many of the leading ideas in later Christian thought about martyrdom are adumbrated here, as well as the central belief that the person who suffers for the gospel receives an outpouring of the Spirit of Jesus Christ. At the same time it is worth noticing that Paul has a remarkably down-to-earth view concerning martyrdom. What matters to him is the mission. It may be furthered either through his own death or through his continuing work for the churches. When he tells his readers that they are full partakers of the grace given to him, it is the grace of his own missionary calling that he has in mind rather than of vocation to a martyr's death. Paul is fully ready to accept death as the consequence of his mission of witness, but he is far from sharing the later ideas of a martyr's death in itself being the goal and crown of discipleship and the supreme mode of union with Christ.

Ephesians 6.19f., whether Pauline or not, reproduces Pauline thinking (as well as that expressed in Acts 4.29–31) when the writer asks his readers to pray that he may receive the gift of speech to make known the mystery (that is, the revelation) of the gospel with παρρησία, and describes himself as an 'ambassador' for the gospel 'in chains'. The 'Paul' of the Pastoral Epistles conveys the same picture of the inspired confessor in rather different terms: 'At my first defence no one took my part . . . But the Lord stood by me and gave me strength to proclaim the word fully, that all the Gentiles might hear it. So I was rescued from the lion's mouth' (II Tim. 4.16f.). So, too, Christians facing persecution are told in I Peter 4.14 that if they are reproached for the name of Christ they are blessed, because 'the Spirit of glory and of God' rests upon them; and the Fourth Gospel repeats the promise given in the synoptic tradition: the warning that disciples will be persecuted is followed by the assurance that the Paraclete, the Spirit of truth, will bear witness to Jesus, and they also are witnesses. It is in their mission that the Paraclete will 'convince the world of sin and of righteousness and of judgment' (John 15.20–26; 16.8).

The negative side of the assurance of inspiration, the extreme seriousness of the sin of apostasy, can also be traced through the New Testament writings. Passages such as Revelation 2.13 and 3.8, which praise those who have stood firm and not 'denied', reveal, as does Hermas, *Sim.* IX,28.4, the anxiety of church leaders lest their people should apostatize, and the warnings in the gospels are echoed in the hymnal fragment quoted in I Timothy 2.12: 'if we endure we shall also reign with him; if we deny him, he also will deny us.' Such denial is a repudiation of a Christian's baptismal allegiance (Rom. 10.9f.), and it involves participation in the corporate denial of Christ that Luke pictures Israel making in Pilate's court (Acts 3.13f.). As the unforgivable blasphemy it evokes the rigorism of the Epistle to the Hebrews (6.4–6; 10.26–31) and of the attitude of I John 5.16 towards the 'sin unto death'.

Two passages relevant to this theme of witness and inspiration deserve special notice. The first is I Timothy 6.12f.:

> Fight the good faith (ἀγῶνα τῆς πίστεως); take hold of the eternal life to which you were called when you made the good confession (ὡμολόγησας τὴν καλὴν ὁμολογίαν) in the presence of many witnesses. In the presence . . . of Christ Jesus who in his testimony (μαρτυρήσαντος) before Pontius Pilate made the good confession, I charge you to keep the commandment unstained and free from reproach.

The view that Timothy is here represented as a confessor in a time of persecution goes back to Theodore of Mopsuestia, who interprets 'you made the good confession' as meaning 'you

suffered',[23] and it has more to be said for it than most commentators allow. It is usually understood to refer to Timothy's
baptismal confession of faith, and ὁμολογεῖν could admittedly
be used to denote this, as it is at Romans 10.9f. It is, however,
most frequently employed in the New Testament to refer to
confession, as opposed to denial, under persecution (Matt.
10.32; Luke 12.8; John 9.22; 12.42; Rev. 3.5), and to the corresponding 'confession' of his faithful disciples by Christ. Further,
the parallel between Timothy's confession in the presence of
many witnesses, which recalls the synoptic allusions to testimony borne before 'governors and kings' and 'to the Gentiles',
and the good confession made by Christ himself before Pilate,
strongly suggests that Timothy's confession, too, was made in
a trial in court. Possibly the reference may be to an actual
historical event; possibly a picture of Timothy as an ideal church
leader is being presented to second-century readers, and is so
designed as to include the element of faithful witness in time
of persecution. In either case the imprisonment of Timothy
implied by Hebrews 13.23 may well be in the writer's mind.

The statement that Jesus witnessed or testified to the good
confession raises other problems. According to the synoptic
traditions, the answer of Jesus to Pilate was no more than: 'You
say [that I am king of the Jews]' (Mark 15.2; Matt. 27.11; Luke
23.3). It is Jesus' silence, rather than any utterance, before Pilate
that the synoptic gospels emphasize. Behind I Timothy 6.13
there may lie a different tradition, possibly also underlying the
Fourth Gospel, of a more extended dialogue than the synoptists
record between Jesus and Pilate; or it is just conceivable that
the author of the Pastorals actually knew the Fourth Gospel and
its story of Jesus' witness to the truth in Pilate's court. The
absence of information in the gospels about any verbal ὁμολογία
made by Jesus before Pilate has prompted a number of exegetes
to interpret the 'good confession' as a synonym for Jesus' actual
death.[24] This is, however, highly unlikely. Although the verb
μαρτυρεῖν passes over from the sense of 'to witness' to that of
'to be a martyr' in such second-century writings as the *Martyrdom of Polycarp* III, 3.4, and Irenaeus, *Adversus Haereses* III, 3.4,
and may be approaching that meaning in I *Clement* 5.3–7, there
seems to be no parallel to the combination of the verb in this
sense with the noun ὁμολογία. The latter never means 'martyrdom' in the sense of a martyr's death as such; it is virtually a
technical term for a martyr's verbal confession of his faith. If in

this case, nevertheless, the phrase did refer to the death of Jesus, ἐπὶ Ποντίου Πιλάτου would have to mean, as in the creeds, 'in the time of Pontius Pilate'. This, too, is unlikely. In the credal formulae that phrase is intended to locate the gospel event in history; here the intention clearly is to state where Jesus made his confession, namely, in Pilate's court. The probability, then, seems to be that Timothy is being represented as a faithful confessor who testified in court, following the example of the Lord.

The remaining passage is the apparently somewhat similar allusion to the μαρτυρία Ἰησοῦ that is the Spirit of prophecy (Rev. 19.10), which I have treated in the previous chapter. To summarize again here, I am unpersuaded by the large number of commentators who urge us to understand the phrase 'the testimony of Jesus' subjectively, as 'the witness borne by Jesus', and that I consider the correct interpretation to be that which takes the genitive objectively, so that the allusion is to 'witness borne to Jesus'. The expression is then parallel to the μαρτύριον τοῦ Κυρίου of II Timothy 1.8, which means 'testimony borne to our Lord' (RSV, 'testifying to our Lord') and closely resembles both the Pauline use of μαρτύριον when it is practically synonymous with εὐαγγέλιον,[25] and also its use by Polycarp when speaking of the 'testimony of [i.e. 'to'] the cross' (*Ep.* 7.1). The objective sense is supported by Revelation (1.2, 9; 12.7; 20.4). On the other hand, the many attempts to explain 'the testimony of Jesus' on the basis of taking the genitive subjectively seem unsuccessful. It is very hard to give a convincing account of what this testimony of Jesus actually was. To suppose that it was not any particular utterance, nor even his teaching as a whole or his general attitude, but rather his death, might be plausible if it could be explained how the death of Jesus, while it might indeed inspire martyrs to die, could be the Spirit of *prophecy*, or be somehow identified with the Holy Spirit. On the other hand, the situation of crisis depicted in the Apocalypse, where the enemies of the faithful are trying to force them to apostatize, is a most appropriate setting for the angel's assurance that it is the Holy Spirit of prophecy that inspires every loyal witness to, or confession of, Jesus. That witness to Jesus is, as it were, the very essence of prophetic inspiration might be taken as a text to sum up the whole theme of the 'pneumatology of martyrdom'.

8

Women and the Ministry of Priesthood

One day near the beginning of this year I dined with someone who claimed that on one unforgettable occasion he had succeeded in falling asleep during his own lecture. I am not sure which is more disconcerting to an audience: to find that the speaker is nodding off, or to be confronted by a lecturer who admits that he, for one, is profoundly bored by his own subject-matter. At one level, the more obvious and superficial level, I must confess that I find the question of the ordination of women to the priesthood almost unbearably tedious. That is because the controversy on this topic in the Church of England has dragged on for the past sixty years or so with endlessly repeated assertions on both sides, yet with little argument adduced by either party with sufficient cogency to convince the other. It has gone on since the days when one of my predecessors, Dr Charles Raven as a young man, and successive Deans of St Paul's, Inge and Matthews, were contending that to admit women to the priesthood was the proper response to the Holy Spirit's guidance of the church in this stage of her history, and when the reply of Sir Robert Newman, MP, the President of the English Church Union in 1921, was the curt, dogmatic, assertion that 'this claim has no possibility of realization since it is flat contrary to the mind of God as revealed in history, and, therefore, equally contrary to the deliberate conviction and practice of the church'. The recent negative decisions of our General Synod make it certain that similar exchanges will continue for quite a long time to come.

Anyone who has followed the recent stages of this war of words is likely to have had more than his fill of repetitious assertions. For my own part, I admit to finding the controversy unexciting and, indeed, depressing, because my own view of the matter, if I may make it clear at the start, is simply this. There are women, some of whom I know personally, who believe that they have been called by God to share in that ministry of his word and sacraments to which I believe that God has called me. The church tested and endorsed my belief. These women are asking the church to test them in the same way. I have no reason at all to think that their conviction is illusory. In other parts of the Anglican Communion of which we are members, as well as in other branches of the church, there are women who have been ordained to this same ministry of God's word and sacraments, and I have met some of them. I have no reason whatever to doubt that the ordination prayer which the church corporately and solemnly prayed for them has been answered and that they have received the Holy Spirit for the office and work of a priest in the church of God. Their ministry is meeting with acceptance and, as much as most priests, they seem to match up to the criterion, 'By their fruits you shall know them'. I have heard no convincing reason why the church should refuse, as the Church of England is continuing to refuse, even to scrutinize and test the belief of these women whom I mentioned, that they have received a vocation to the priesthood, and I do not think that this negative attitude helps to further the cause of the kingdom of God or to commend it to the generality of mankind. So I should like the church to get on and ordain them and be quit of a controversy which seems to me to be unnecessary, distracting, and tiresome.

At this level, then, I find the subject a great bore. But at another, deeper, level the controversy is very far from tedious. It should be intensely interesting to theologians (and everyone who tries to think about the implications of his or her faith is a theologian). For although to admit women to the priesthood seems to some of us to be no more than a natural and obvious step for us to take, and nothing to make a fuss about, the sharp controversy, and the deeply and sincerely felt opposition that has been aroused, raise very many of the most fundamental questions in the wider contemporary theological debate. Among the proximate issues in this controversy are the questions: What is priesthood? What is the relation of the corporate priesthood of the whole church to particular ministerial offices? What is meant and signified and effected by ordination? What should be the relation of the ministry of the word to the ministry of the sacraments? The whole question of authority in the church is raised: if tradition, whether in doctrine, ethics, or worship, is always affected by the relativities of history, what value or authority has it for our own culturally-conditioned beliefs, ethics and modes of worship? What is the authority of the writings canonized as 'Holy Scripture', in view of the fact that biblical criticism has shown that they, too, are in no way exempt from historical relativity?

Such questions lead us on – I cannot now enumerate the many issues that this raises, outside the specifically theological sphere, in the areas of anthropology, psychology and sociology – to the more remote but still more basic problems of what we mean by revelation, and whether timeless truths are ever and anywhere available to us, and in the end, when we ask such questions as whether Jesus may be supposed to have laid down any kind of blueprint for the future ordering of his church, and, more importantly, whether, if he did, this should necessarily remain binding upon ourselves after two thousand years of history, we move from questions of history to the most fundamental issues of christology. To a very considerable extent, it would seem, the actual question of the priesthood of women is but the tip of a much larger, still not completely visible, iceberg of controversy, or, to change the metaphor, it serves to trigger off those much more far-reaching disputes which are really dividing thinking Christians from one another at the present time, across the old party lines and denominational boundaries: disputes about the nature of revelation and, hence, about authority in religion, the extent to which we can speak, if at all, of revealed doctrines or a 'Faith once delivered to the saints', and of unchanging norms of belief embodied in the classical creeds: disputes, in the last resort, about the nature of God's relationship to his human creation, in Jesus and universally. It is, I think, because people discern, however dimly, behind this particular controversy, the major issues that divide liberal Christianity from traditionalist Christianity, that feeling has become so surprisingly intense, and party strife, which had seemed for years to be almost dormant in the Church of England, has revived with quite unexpected vigour. In relation to this more profound division, the ordination of women is perhaps playing a somewhat similar role to that of the Latin Mass in Archbishop Lefebvre's movement of protest.

What is it that we mean when we talk about priesthood? The

language which we use in this connection is derived, through the entire Christian tradition, from the Old Testament. Whatever else may be implied by priesthood, it would be agreed that it expresses two central ideas: that of a human being who is in some way commissioned and empowered by God to declare his law, that is to say, to be a channel of God's communication to his people, and to be a representative agent through whom God's people offer their response of worship, prayer, praise, and the total self-dedication and service which in the religion of the Old Testament was symbolized concretely by the offering of material sacrifices and in later Judaism, as in Philo, and in Christianity, as in Rom. 12.1, is understood to mean the consecration of ourselves for the service of God. Adam, everyman, is thus intended by God to be a priestly character; for the priest's role is to mediate, and man is created to be the agent of God's providential care for the material world and all the creatures in it, and to represent the world and the whole of the lower creation in praising their maker and serving his creative purposes. Christ is seen by Paul and by the writer to the Hebrews, and by the whole subsequent Christian tradition, as the true Adam, the ideal and archetypal human being, and as the universal high priest, mediating the grace and love of God to the world and summing up in himself the dedication and obedience to the loving creativity of God which the human creation owes to the Creator. In the Old Testament the mediating role of Adam is focused in the covenant people of Israel, a people called to be priests, to mediate God to the nations and the nations to God, and when this mission had been at last concretely embodied and carried out by Jesus, who represents both Adam and Israel, his Spirit passed on to the community of his followers, so that they became the true Israel, a priestly community, representing humanity in its relation to God and communicating God to mankind as a channel of his love. It is always worth remembering that it is in these two connections, and these only, that the New Testament writers speak of priests and priesthood in a Christian context: Christ, and by derivation from him, the community of Christian people.

Anglican theology has generally derived what is often called the ministerial priesthood from the priesthood of Christ in which, by grace and in total dependence upon his Spirit, the church corporately participates. I think it is very important that we should continue to think of priesthood along these lines, and it seems unfortunate that the Anglican–Roman Catholic International Commission's agreed statement on the ministry[1] is ambiguous on this point. After expounding the notion of priesthood in terms of Christ and the church, and apparently setting out to deduce the ministerial priesthood from the priesthood of the whole society that is the body of Christ, the statement interposes an obscure sentence, which has been much criticized, to the effect that the ministerial priesthood is not derived from the corporate priesthood but is of a different order. This is most unfortunate, for I am sure that the only way in which we can arrive at a satisfactory understanding of the nature of the ordained or ministerial priesthood is to see it as the representative organ and, if you like, the central executive agency of the community as a whole which is itself a priestly body, indwelt and inspired by the Spirit of Christ, the priestly mediator of God to man and man to God. This does not mean that ordained priests are mere delegates, appointed by the congregation for convenience's sake to act on their behalf. We should all agree that they are called and appointed and empowered by God acting through his people, by the voice and hands of their representatives who are his own representatives. It is often said that the priesthood of the ordained minister differs from that of the church as a whole in that the church exercises its ministry towards the rest of the world, mediating God to it and it to God, whereas the ministerial priest exercises his priesthood towards the church itself. This is partly true; but the so-called lay member of the priestly community may exercise all kinds of Christ-like ministries towards his fellow Christians, while the ordained minister may find himself spear-heading the church's ministry to those outside its membership. The distinction between lay and clerical Christians is, of course, entirely absent from the church of the New Testament period, and its introduction during the early centuries seems to have caused a confusion about priesthood from which it is extremely hard to extricate ourselves. The confusion was greatly increased when the vocation to certain forms of ministry was held to involve a call to celibacy, thus dividing laity and clergy almost into two different species of humanity. We have to remember that ministry, according to Paul's understanding of it, was extremely diversified and shared by all the members of the Christian body. Each person had his particular gift, or special operation of God's

Spirit, to use for the building up of the community: prophecy, healing, teaching, administration, and so on.

All this is relevant and important to our question. From the start women were admitted to full membership of the priestly society. This is the remarkable advance beyond the relative subordination of women in Judaism which Paul expresses when he says that in Christ there is neither Jew nor Gentile, bond nor free, male nor female. He is, of course, talking about membership of the church, not directly about ordination but rather about baptism. But what he says has implications for ministerial priesthood, for if that priesthood is a representative nucleus, focal point, spearhead, or whatever image may best describe it, of the priesthood of the whole body which consists equally of men and women, it is hard to see why the women members should be excluded from the ministerial priesthood which represents them and acts as their agent. In fact the more positive question arises, whether the ministerial priesthood can be properly representative of the priestly community unless it does include women.

Women, of course, may and do participate in many ministries such as those which Paul enumerates in Rom. 12 and I Cor. 12. They do teach, heal, administer, and use the gifts which God's Spirit gives them so as to build up the community to be the body of Christ. In our Anglican situation these ministries include the ministry of God's word, than which there is no higher form of ministry, for it is the gospel which constitutes the church, and the preaching of the good news of Christ is the essential apostolic ministry of which Paul spoke when, referring to himself and Apollos and other missionaries, he said, 'Let a man so account of us as of the ministers of Christ and stewards of the mysteries of God' (I Cor. 4.1). Until recent times, when the ministry of women was under discussion, the picture in most people's minds was of a woman occupying the pulpit. Now, however, this is accepted. Women do preach, and the days are long past when a woman preacher was expected to give her sermon from some inconvenient place on the floor of the church, the pulpit being reserved for the official, ordained, minister of the word. The ministry of God's word involves much besides public preaching: teaching, counselling, and other personal forms of ministry to individuals. The woman reader or deaconess does all this, and the church, in encouraging her to do so and giving her its authorization, has plainly implied that it considers the attitude of the early church, expressed in I Cor. 14.34f. and I Tim. 2.11f., forbidding a woman to teach and telling her to keep silence in the congregation, to be culturally determined and irrelevant to the entirely different circumstances of the present day. This means that those prooftexts for the tradition which has excluded women from the priesthood all down the ages are no longer relevant to the discussion. In our Anglican situation we are left with the extraordinary result that what is at stake is simply whether women should continue to be excluded from the presidency at the eucharist, that is to say, from saying the eucharistic prayer (they may already lead much of the service and give communion to the people), and continue to be excluded from formally taking responsibility for a cure of souls, despite the fact that a woman may be put in temporary charge of a parish or act in the place of a vicar in a team ministry.

Anglican tradition, since the Reformation, has laid stress on the close connection between the word and the sacraments, though it has often failed badly to establish this in practice. Perhaps the best and most lasting effect of the Anglo–Catholic movement has been to vindicate the centrality of the eucharist in Sunday worship, and under the influence of the liturgical movement this has been balanced by a renewed emphasis on the importance of the sermon in the eucharistic liturgy. The exclusion of women from the priesthood has meant that in their case a new dichotomy has been created between the word, which they may minister, and the sacrament, which they may not. The same objection might rightly be raised to the ministry of male readers, or indeed, of deacons, and this is a reason for preferring part-time priests to lay readers; but the objection is much less strong in their case, for it is open to a male reader to seek ordination to the priesthood, and normal for a deacon to do so, whereas for a woman the restriction to a non-sacramental ministry of the word is permanent. So we have the anomaly that a woman may perhaps preside over a religious community or a college or school, yet she may not preside at the eucharist which is the corporate offering of her own community. Similarly, because the ministry of absolution is restricted to the priest, a woman may engage in a ministry of counselling to the point where she may believe that there is an urgent need to declare authoritative absolution; but at that point she has to tell the person concerned to go to a male priest outside that particular intimate pastoral situation. This is particularly anomalous because many Anglicans would regard this ministry less as a sacrament than as a particular form of the ministry of the word; she may declare God's forgiveness publicly in preaching but not privately in the word of absolution.

It is not easy to say why a person needs to be ordained a priest in order to say the eucharistic prayer but not in order to preach the word. Classical Protestantism would be reluctant to admit that a preacher need not be an ordained minister, but we have accepted this. We therefore have to ask what ordination signifies. I cannot attempt to answer this question here. It is very difficult to find an answer. We can certainly say that in ordination the church acknowledges the ministry of the person ordained, so that he can thenceforward speak and act with the church's authority and in its name as its representative. It implies a degree of commitment to ministry on his part, greater that that demanded of a lay worker. It need not be full time, but it is assumed to be life-long and to be that form of service to which this person's life is primarily dedicated. Ordination is not merely an act of recognition and acknowledgment, but of prayer and of the divine answer to prayer in the gift of the grace of God's Spirit for the carrying out of this ministry. Nothing is involved in this which seems to restrict ordination to male persons.

The controversy about the ordination of women has thrown up a new and very different conception of priesthood. According to this, priesthood is not a focusing of the church's corporate priesthood upon an individual who represents the whole body. It is rather a gift by which God enables certain individuals to represent Christ to the church. Because Christ incarnate was male, these individuals must also be male. Although all Christians are being transformed by God's Spirit into the likeness of Christ, the priest embodies the divine initiative and love, in response to which all other Christians may be thus transformed. So the priest is an icon of Christ, a sacrament in himself through whom Christ is made present to his people in the eucharist. He is the icon of Christ as the new Adam, through whom new life enters the world; the congregation, though they receive that new life and may themselves become channels of it to the rest of the world, receive it through the priest as its initiator.

This idea of priesthood has no place, so far as I am aware, in ancient tradition, and it has come into Anglican thinking from modern Orthodoxy. It is open to grave objections. First, it reflects a theology which gives too little place to the Spirit of God; for it is the Spirit, not the priest, who makes Christ present to us and who initiates and carries through the transformation of ourselves into the likeness of Christ. Secondly, although the most elementary teaching about ordination has always told us that the priest is not a higher-grade Christian than the lay person and that ordination does not as such make him a better man or closer to God, this theory clearly implies that there is a difference in kind between the priesthood of the whole community and the priesthood of the ordained man. He becomes a mediator between God and man in a sense which a good theology of church and ministry has always repudiated. Thirdly, although the priest represents Christ, he does this as a representative, not as a representation. An ambassador represents the Queen. He acts in her name; he speaks for her; he is her representative; but he is not a representation of the Queen. He does not impersonate her. He need not be a woman; nor when a queen succeeds a king do all the sovereign's representatives have to be replaced, if they are men, by women. This notion that a priestly representative of Christ must be male rests on a failure to understand the use of analogy and poetic symbolism in religious language. Ignatius (*Trallians* 3.1) saw the deacon as a type of Christ (incidentally, this did not seem to the early church to imply that a woman could not be a deacon), and the bishop as a type of God the Father. But Ignatius was not using the language of literal description, but of poetic symbolism. 'Father' is an analogy which illuminates basic aspects of God's dealings with us; but it does not mean that God is literally a Father, a masculine person. Hence, fourthly, the priest must resemble the historical Jesus, the male person, in so far as he needs to do what Christ did, such as to take bread and break and say words of thanksgiving. But these are human actions, not specifically masculine actions, and since the priest is not playing the part of Christ in the sense in which this is done at Oberammergau, there is no reason at all why a woman cannot represent him. It is not, finally, Christ's maleness but his humanity in the image of which we are being renewed and into which we are incorporated. According to classical christology, God the Word took human nature, the nature common to both men and women. Of course he had to be either a man or a woman, and in the circumstances of the time his mission required him to be a man, but if this were christologically significant the female half of mankind would not be redeemed. Professor R. A. Norris, in a paper for the Anglican–Roman Catholic consultation, says:

> The maleness of Jesus is of no christological interest in patristic tradition . . . it never occurred to the fathers to make any more play with Jesus' sex than they did with his race. 'He became human that we might become divine', says one of them. And presumably this 'we', and therefore this humanity, includes women. To make of the maleness of Christ a christological principle is to qualify or deny the universality of his redemption.[2]

Christ is indeed pictured as the bridegroom, as he is also pictured as the shepherd, the vine and the door. The church is pictured as his bride. Yet the priest represents the church as well as Christ. It is a total misuse of analogy and symbolism to say either that a woman priest cannot represent Christ because he is the bridegroom or that a man priest cannot represent the church because it is the bride.

The tradition of the church is solidly against the ordination of women, not in the sense that it has followed negative rulings given after full consideration of the matter, but that this has never been done and it has always been assumed that it was out of the question. What is the weight and value of this negative tradition? It might be thought to measure up closely to the Vincentian canon: *quod semper, quod ubique, quod ab omnibus*. But we must remember that this canon applied to what is believed: to faith rather than practice, and if we were really bound to exclude from our thought and life everything that has not been thought and lived out 'always', 'everywhere', 'by all Christians', we should rule out the possibility of all change in the church; nothing could ever happen in it for the first time. This is manifestly absurd, and is contradicted by history. There have been great and frequent changes in the church's belief, ethics, worship and structures. Nor must we forget that the church's attitudes are always affected by the culture of particular times and places; that this applies even to the decisions of ecumenical councils, and that, incidentally, the ancient councils were never really ecumenical in the sense of world-wide. Almost all the participants shared the culture and outlook of the Roman Empire. Even if it were possible to unite the churches and refer this question to an ecumenical council today, we could not hope that agreement would be reached in a body embracing the Western peoples, where to take this step is often seen as a natural concomitant of the roles played by women in other spheres of Christian service, and African Christians to whom at present it would appear unnatural and offensive.

We have to look at the presuppositions underlying the tradition. They are those which caused the medieval theologians to formulate the doctrine that women are inherently incapable of receiving the sacrament of orders, namely, that women, because of their natural state of subjection, lack that 'eminence of degree' which is requisite for priesthood. According to Duns Scotus even the Mother of the Lord, greatly as she is to be venerated, shared in the natural inferiority that inescapably belongs to her sex. That is why, he says, repeating an idea that goes back to Epiphanius, she was not permitted to baptize her son and so he had to receive baptism from John. When we ask for the evidence of this inferiority of women, the answer, apart from a glance at Aristotle's dictum that 'a female is, so to speak, a deformed male' (which Aristotle thought was a scientific observation) turns out to be based on Gen. 3.16 ('Thy desire shall be to thy husband and he shall rule over thee'), and I Tim. 2.12, which forbids women to teach and to lord it over men. Some people argue that the text of Genesis was misused in the tradition: it refers to the relation of woman to man in the fallen state of the human race, and ought not to apply to the order of redemption. But we surely ought not to discuss it uncritically as though we were not aware that there never was an actual fall or an actual creation on the lines portrayed in Genesis. In any case, the text of I Timothy is irrelevant to the present controversy, since it is concerned to stop women from teaching, which our church encourages them to do, and the text of Genesis, even mythologically interpreted, would only be relevant if we really believed that women are naturally in a state of subordination to men which unfits them for the exercise of 'headship'. Very few, however, of those who debar women from priesthood on the ground that this would be a contravention of the subordination of women, which they profess to believe is built into the order of creation, follow the logic of the argument and object to the headship of women in all other spheres of life, outside the church as well as inside. This also raises the question whether the priestly ministry really does, or at any rate whether it ought to, involve dominance or pater-

nalism. The teaching and example of Jesus strongly suggest that
it should not.

Scripture is misused again when it is said that since Jesus
included no women among the Twelve, the church must follow
his example and ordain no women to the priesthood. It is
alleged that his exclusion of women from the apostolate is significant in view of his highly original and unconventional regard
for, and friendship with, women. But there is no evidence at
all that the early church took the choice of the Twelve as in any
sense a model or blueprint for its own ministry of presbyters
and deacons. If it had, then when Samaritan and Gentiles were
added to the church (not without doubts and controversies),
Jewish Christians might well have used the same arguments
that are now being propounded about Jesus' choice of the
Twelve. 'Jesus,' they might have said, 'showed quite extraordinary friendship to these people. But he never chose one of
them to join the Twelve. The fact that they were all Jews is very
significant. It implies that, although Samaritans and Gentiles
may certainly be baptized into the church, to allow them to be
ordained as presbyters would be to disregard the clear intention
of the Lord.' But no one said anything of the kind. The Twelve
had a unique role. They were chosen to be the symbolical
founder-patriarchs of the twelve tribes of the renewed and reformed Israel: 'When the Son of man shall sit on his glorious
throne, you . . . will also sit on twelve thrones, judging the
twelve tribes of Israel' (Matt. 19.28). No one would deny that
one thing a woman cannot be is a patriarch. After the first
Easter they became missionary-pioneers, witnesses to the end
of the earth. That was not a possible task for women at that
time. The participation of women on that kind of scale and at
that sort of level, whether in church or society generally, has
only been made possible through the effects of the industrial
revolution, particularly in the developed countries; in many
parts of the world the situation is still not unlike that of the first
century. To suggest that Jesus could have instituted a female
apostolate had he wished to do so is to imply that he could
have first carried through a total economic, and consequently
social, revolution. (The priestesses of the pagan cults represent
an entirely different kind of institution and cannot be brought
into a comparison with the early Christian ministry, in which
there were no priests, either, as Jews or pagans understood the
term.) But, also, we must not forget that he was himself a Jew.

His own revolutionary attitudes were still contained within the framework of Jewish belief and practice. Not only would he recognize that a mixed apostolate would be quite unacceptable to his contemporaries, but he may well have shared their view, despite his striking individual friendships with women. We need not now share that view ourselves, for the Spirit of Christ leads us in some areas beyond the beliefs of Jesus himself in his own time. Further, this whole argument begs the major question whether Jesus intended to found a church, or whether, on the one hand, he expected his death to bring in the Parousia immediately, or, on the other, he had in view a continuing community but in the form not of a new church but rather of a renewed and purified, yet continuous, Israel. The probabilities of these alternatives are surely in inverse order to that in which I have set them out. It was the Spirit of God rather than Jesus in the days of his flesh who founded the Catholic Church. It is a pre-critical misconception to suppose, therefore, that he laid down a plan for its structure and ordering. Nor, even if he had done this, would it necessarily be right to maintain it unchanged in the totally different circumstances of the present century. Any argument that, if Jesus himself determined the organization of the church, it must be maintained unchanged for all time because he is God and omniscient, rests on the same kind of false, ultimately docetic, christology which, before Bishop Gore's *Lux Mundi* and his *Dissertations on the Incarnation*, caused people to think that, if Jesus attributed a psalm to David, that settled the question of its authorship because he is God and therefore knows.

It has often been said recently, especially by Orthodox thinkers, that it belongs peculiarly to a male person to symbolize the divine initiative of self-giving love which was communicated by Jesus to his people on the cross and which is re-presented in the eucharist. It is the recipient church which may appropriately be symbolized by a woman. This is ultimately a sexual analogy, and one which seems to have become quite disproportionately exaggerated. A mother may surely be as potent a symbol of unselfish and self-sacrificing love as a husband; so, indeed, may a wife. Symbols change; the image of the shepherd becomes almost unintelligible in an urban society; the father image no longer speaks to us in its old terms; the symbolism of male and female changes with the development of equal partnership. In so far as either a man or a woman symbolize God and his attributes through their actual sexuality, it is surely much more in the pulpit where a person's individual personality is emphasized, and where, let us not forget, Christ is also truly present and communicated, than at the altar where, especially in Catholic tradition, the individual celebrant is as anonymous and impersonal as possible. The recent Orthodox stress on the priest as icon seems to represent an unfortunate break with this tradition.

Of course it is said that all these theological issues are in the last resort a smoke-screen. What the churches that have ordained women are doing is simply following secular fashion and working out the ideas of the women's liberation movement in the ecclesiastical sphere. This is not so. There is a secular background to the movement for the priesthood of women, but it is much more profound and important than the ideas of the campaigners for women's rights. It is no less than the fundamental economic and social changes which have transformed the lives of all men and women in the industrial world. This mighty revolution, which cannot be reversed, makes all the stream of tradition that belongs to the pre-revolutionary world out of date: not that all of it has to be discarded, but all of it has to be examined and rethought. The ordination of women is seen, in this society, as the natural conclusion, for Christian people, of the changes in the roles of women that this revolution has made possible during the last century and a quarter. We should be cautious about using the word 'secular' to describe these changes. They do not come about without God's providence. God speaks to the church through the world as well as to the world through the church, and it is through the interaction of the church with the world that we may, if we listen, hear God's word.

9

The 'Limuru Principle' and Church Unity

At its first meeting at Limuru in 1971 the Anglican Consultative Council declared that:

> In considering full communion with the Church of South India, the Council has given some thought to the questions which will arise with the future formation and development of united Churches, of which Churches not hitherto episcopally ordered form a part. These questions do not permit simple solutions. Anglican Churches have always regarded episcopal ordination as a necessary element in any Church with which they can have full communion. The question of ordination, however, cannot be treated in isolation. In any episcopally ordered Church the minister who presides at ordination will of course always be a bishop. But the act of ordination is only rightly understood if it is seen within the context of the entire sacramental and pastoral ministry of the bishop. It is as the father of the family, as the leader of its worship and witness, and as its chief pastor that the bishop also presides at the service of ordination.
>
> In the CSI all the clergy in a diocese form one family in full communion with the bishop, sharing with him in one common liturgical life and acting under his pastoral leadership. It may therefore fairly be said that they form one episcopally ordered ministry, even though some of them were originally ordained otherwise than by the laying on of the bishop's hands. It would seem clear that this is in fact the way in which CSI itself regards its ministry. The question arises whether Anglican Churches should accept this view of the matter, and be ready to accept this anomaly within the process of reunion.[1]

The importance of the Limuru statement

The potential importance of this statement is very great. If the theory of the church, the ministry, and episcopal order which it implies can come to be generally accepted, the present depressing state of inter-church relations can be radically and speedily transformed. Immense changes for the better in ecumenical relationships have taken place during recent years. There has been a most striking development not only of good will, co-operation in mission, and joint pastoral activity, but also of intercommunion, with or without official sanction. Nevertheless, the goal which was originally aimed at by most Anglicans, organic union, is still far off, and it looks as though the coming together of the United Reformed Church in this country will remain the exception which throws into strong relief the continuing failure of the Church of England, for all its traditional insistence that the churches ought to settle for nothing less than organic union, actually to achieve it with any other Christian body. The chief reason for this failure, as the United Reformed success reminds us, is, of course, the difficulty of uniting episcopal with non-episcopal ministries; and here the Limuru statement points a way forward beyond the present impasse.

The context of the statement is a short discussion of full communion with the Church of South India. Unfortunately, earlier in the report, the Council had spoken of 'full communion' in a way which created a precedent for confusion and ambiguity and which, to some extent, blunted the impact of its subsequent statement about episcopal ordination. 'Full communion,' as the term had come to be used in ecumenical discussion, for instance in *Intercommunion Today*,[2] is a relationship between two or more churches, intermediate between the stage of 'partial communion' which involves not only intercommunion but also mutual recognition and interchangeability of ministries. The churches concerned still retain their separate identities; their memberships and their organizations remain distinct, but they stand in a similar relationship to each other as was planned for Anglicans and Methodists in England at Stage I and, indeed, as the churches of the Anglican Communion enjoy among themselves. At Limuru, however, a badly misconceived warning was issued against a 'too rigid definition of full communion'. It was suggested that between the Church of South India and other churches 'full communion may lack completeness when a Church has a rule confining the ministration of the sacraments to an episcopally ordained ministry'; it was also stated that 'full communion between an Anglican Province and the Churches of North India and Pakistan may be limited by the requirement of those Churches that ministers who go to serve in them shall take part in the Rite of Unification of Ministries'.

This was altogether perverse. Full communion that 'lacks completeness' is obviously not full. It is partial communion. This was an attempt to have the cake of full communion and at the same time to eat it by introducing a limitation in the shape of 'local rules' that may exclude non-episcopally ordained ministers of one of the churches that are supposed to be in full communion with each other from ministering the sacraments in another of these churches. It has already been used by the General Synod to enable the Church of England to appear to be in full communion with the Church of South India while limiting the recognition and interchangeability of ministries so as to exclude from it the non-episcopally ordained ministers of the Church of South India. This was disingenuous, not to say dishonest. The dishonesty is not intentional; it is caused by the desire, common in ecumenical dialogue and very dangerous, to avoid giving offence even at the cost of truth. To refuse to enter into full communion with another church seems offensive; so we establish full communion with it, but since we cannot really enter into full communion in the proper sense of the term we resort to the explanation that our domestic regulations entail that this must be a 'full communion' that must 'lack completeness'.

This disastrous ambiguity takes the edge off the Limuru statement about full communion with the Church of South India. If, however, the term 'full communion' can be taken to mean no less than what it says, the implications of the statement are highly important. Anglican churches, as it points out, have always regarded episcopal ordination as a necessary element in any church with which they can have full communion. The question remains, however, whether 'episcopal ordination' in this context is synonymous with the 'episcopal ordering of the Ministry'. The Lambeth Quadrilateral laid it down that acceptance of the historic episcopal ministry is a necessary condition for union with the Church of England, and the re-expression of this principle in the Lambeth Appeal of 1920 and in the subsequent explanations of the terms of the Appeal did not materially alter its force. Full communion involving interchangeability of ministries has required the fulfilment of the same condition or of an alternative which, like the rite of unification in the Anglican-Methodist Scheme, is susceptible of an interpretation which would equate it with episcopal ordination. Acceptance of the historic episcopal ministry, however, need not necessarily mean that every minister of a church which accepts it must either have been originally ordained by a bishop or receive episcopal ordination, or an equivalent rite, before full communion or union is inaugurated. The discussion of conditions for intercommunion offers a certain parallel: many Anglicans who would otherwise think that episcopal ordination of all the ministers of the other church concerned would be a precondition for corporate intercommunion are prepared to grant that intercommunion with a non-episcopal church can be justified if there is a real desire on the part of the other church to aim at organic union with the Anglican church and so to become episcopally ordered in the not too distant future. Not all the individual ministers as yet, but the church itself, is to become episcopally ordered, and even the intention, though still at present unfulfilled, is held to alter the non-episcopal character of the church concerned.

The Church of England and the historic episcopate

If it is possible for a church to be episcopally ordered, even though not all its ministers have received episcopal ordination, the question which the Church of England has to face is *why* it insists on acceptance of the historic episcopate as a pre-requisite for full communion, and *a fortiori* for organic union. This is not an easy question to answer, precisely because the Church of England has always been reluctant to commit itself to any one particular theory of episcopacy. It has been content to maintain a strict invariability of practice in its own internal order. For the purpose of preserving Anglican unity it is enough that every minister shall have received his ordination to the diaconate and the priesthood from a canonically consecrated bishop possessing authority to ordain; there is no need to ask questions about the doctrinal basis of this rule, nor to enquire what its implications may be concerning the status of non-episcopally ordained ministers in other churches. It is only when the Church of England becomes engaged in a serious consideration of its relations with other churches that it finds itself compelled to answer questions about the doctrine of episcopacy. Unless the other churches concerned are episcopally ordered in the sense that they not only possess bishops in the historic succession but also that their ministers, without exception, have been episcopally ordained, these questions can no longer be evaded under cover of uniformity of practice. We have to ask the decisive, and unhappily divisive, question whether 'episcopal order' is or is not to be interpreted as entailing the ordination by a bishop of every minister in a church so ordered.

According to a theory of apostolic succession such as that which was made familiar by the Tractarians, the answer is affirmative. The reason why union or full communion is possible only with an episcopally ordered church is that a non-episcopally ordered church has no priests. The authority and grace to execute the office and work of a priest in the church of God are derived from Christ through his commissioning and empowering of the apostles, through transmission by them to the bishops as their successors, and so through the episcopal succession down the ages. It is thus the succession of the historic ministry which constitutes and preserves the church; for where there are no bishops in the apostolic succession there can be no authentic ministers of the word and the sacraments. As J. M. Neale expressed it:

> So age by age, and year by year,
>   His grace was handed on;
> And still the holy Church is here,
>   Although her Lord is gone.

Nowadays there are few defenders of Neale's theory of episcopacy. The historical assertions on which it was based are generally recognized as belonging to a pre-critical and anachronistic conception of Christian origins; and it is interesting to see how completely these assertions have been discarded in the Anglican–Roman Catholic agreement on the ministry. Nor is there any need today to labour the obvious theological objections to Neale's idea that Christ is absent, but the church is still here because the ministry, in succession to Christ through his apostles, acts as *vicarius Christi*, usurping the role of the Holy Spirit. The 'pipeline' theory of the transmission of grace in ordination has often enough been discredited by unanswerable theological and historical arguments, and no attempt to restate it in terms less obviously objectionable than Neale's caricature-like hymn has been at all successful. Nevertheless, the Church of England continues, as a body, to act as though it still believes that theory to be true. Its policy towards other churches would sometimes be inexplicable unless it held that 'episcopal order' involved the ordination of every minister either by his own bishop or by another, in the historic succession. This is the principle, unstated in the official resolutions, which alone makes intelligible the present relationship of the Church of England to the Church of South India: full communion which nevertheless 'lacks completeness' because no exception has been made in favour of the non-episcopally ordained presbyters of the Church of South India to the law which restricts sacramental ministry within the Church of England to priests who have received ordination from a bishop in the historic succession. The official explanation is simply that the local rules of the Church of England impose this unavoidable limitation on full communion; but this is purely legalistic: the reason why it has so far been deemed inexpedient to create an exception to the local rules is the theological conviction that a non-episcopally ordained minister, even though he may serve in an episcopally governed church, is not an authentic minister of the sacraments.

Limuru issued a welcome reminder that episcopal order admits of another interpretation. Thereby it forces us to clarify our thinking about the theory that underlies our uniformity of practice. Is our refusal to acknowledge the interchangeability of non-episcopal with episcopal ministries due to a continuing belief, notwithstanding the arguments that have been directed towards its refutation, that the former represent a break in the 'pipeline' and that consequently they cannot possess the grace and authority to celebrate the sacrament which is authentically Christ's and the church's eucharist? Or, on the other hand, is our refusal due not so much to a belief that these individual ministers have not received Christ's grace in ordination as to a conviction that the historic episcopate is an effective sign and seal of the unity and continuity of the church, and that, in consequence, the ministries which lack episcopal ordination are signs of schism and disunity? On the latter view, it is not primarily the sacramental status of the particular minister which is the question at issue: that is to say, his possession or lack of a transmitted grace of orders. The question ultimately refers, rather, to the church. If the bishop is the focus and the outward sign of the unity of the Christian church, must not a minister who claims to have been ordained to the church's ministry by some person or persons other than a bishop break the unity of the church when he celebrates the eucharist? His ordination, on this view, represents not a break in the 'pipeline', but a breach of unity, making it impossible to regard him as an authentic minister of the church and to treat his ministry as interchangeable with that of an episcopally ordained priest.

A theory similar to the latter is implied in the Limuru statement. It points out that the ministry of a bishop comprises much more than ordination. Ordination cannot be treated in isolation. It must be seen within the 'entire sacramental and pastoral ministry of the bishop'. The suggestion is that when ordination is set within this broad perspective it can cease to be the decisive factor. What makes a church's ministry to be 'episcopally ordered' is not the episcopal ordination of every one of its individual ministers, but the fact that they are all in communion with the bishop, acting under his authority and sharing with him in the church's common liturgical life. If all the ministers of a church are in this relationship of communion with the bishop, are subject to his jurisdiction, and serve under his authority, then that church is episcopally ordered, whether or not they were all themselves originally ordained by a bishop.

Communion with the bishop

The question, then, is first of all what is meant by a minister of a church being 'in communion with' his bishop. It might be argued that in the case of a layman 'communion with the bishop' is established by confirmation, and in the case of a clergyman by ordination. Some such interpretation may seem to be implied by our strange practice of using confirmation as a rite of reception into the Church of England of members of non-episcopal churches, even if they are already mature and advanced communicants, confirmed long ago in their own churches. There is, however, increasing dissatisfaction with this practice. There is also a strong feeling in many quarters that confirmation need not be treated as a necessary preliminary to admission to communicant status within our own membership. Communion with the bishop, it would seem, is established primarily through membership of a parish or other congregation of which the bishop is the chief pastor and the leader of mission, the local minister of which celebrates communion as, in theory, the bishop's deputy and representative. Communion with the bishop, on this view, is not to be referred only to a layman's initiation into adult and responsible church membership by the rite of confirmation; it is a continuing relationship, formed and expressed in the bishop's continuing pastoral ministry and the on-going worship and mission of the entire local Christian community in its relation to him. Similarly, the communion of a clergyman with his bishop should not be referred only to his initiation as a minister by the rite of ordination, but to his continuing relationship with the bishop as his chief pastor and the leader in worship and mission under whose authority and guidance he carries out his own ministry; communion with the bishop is a relationship which he shares with the church as a whole.

The further question is whether a clergyman's communion with the bishop can actually be held to be established in some circumstances apart from, and without, the relationship created by ordination. It would seem that it can. If a layman can come to be in communion with the bishop without having been episcopally confirmed (as most schemes of union presuppose), it is reasonable to suppose that a clergyman can come to be in communion with the bishop without having been episcopally ordained. This, as the Limuru statement points out, is the way in which the Church of South India itself regards its non-episcopally ordained clergy. There is a similar precondition, however, in each case. It must be presupposed that a person who has not been episcopally confirmed can nevertheless be acknowledged to be a fully initiated layman in the church. It must also be recognized that a minister who has been ordained non-episcopally can nevertheless be fully acknowledged to be a true minister of the word and sacraments in the universal church of Christ.

If an episcopally ordained clergyman from elsewhere becomes one of the clergy in a diocese who 'form one family in full communion with the bishop', acting under the bishop's authority and representing him in the local situation, his relationship to the bishop is formally expressed through the granting to him of the bishop's licence. A non-episcopally ordained clergyman in an episcopally ordered church, formed in accordance with the Church of South India pattern, would similarly be licensed to act under the bishop's authority and with his backing and guidance. Licensing does not, however, in any sense take the place of ordination and in itself make a man a minister of the word and sacraments. A man cannot be licensed unless he has first been ordained. The theory that a person can enter into communion with the bishop by being, in effect, licensed by him to work as a minister under his authority, therefore rests upon the prior acknowledgment that such a person is already in fact a minister of the word and sacraments. If a non-episcopally ordained minister can receive from the bishop a status that corresponds to his being licensed, this presupposes that he is already recognized as being as authentic a minister of the word and sacraments in and of the universal church of Christ as his episcopally ordained colleagues. If he is this, and is therefore truly a minister and not a layman, he can receive the bishop's authorization to represent him and to exercise his ministry within the bishop's jurisdiction and under his direction. The 'Limuru principle' thus rests on the presupposition that the former ministers of non-episcopal churches who have come to serve in a united episcopal church were made true ministers of the word and sacraments by their (non-episcopal) ordination.

The obstacle to union

The obstacle, therefore, that must be overcome if full communion or organic union is to be achieved between an Anglican church and the church to which such ministers belong is not, according to the Limuru principle, a belief that non-episcopally ordained ministers have really received no ordination at all, but are properly to be regarded as laymen. According to a strict interpretation of the 'Tractarian' doctrine of priesthood and episcopacy this would in fact be the case. These ministers would be really laymen; they would not have received Christ's authority and commission, bestowed exclusively through ordination by a bishop in the historic succession, to minister the word and the sacraments, and they would not have received the grace of orders, transmitted from Christ through the apostles and the bishops who are their successors. There is then only one remedy for their deficiency, which can make them into true ministers of Christ's church: ordination by a bishop standing in the apostolic succession. Until they have received ordination at the hands of the bishop they cannot become members of the 'family' of his clergy or receive authority to act on his behalf; for they are not priests.

The Limuru statement assumes that the obstacle to union is of a different kind from this. What is at present keeping the churches apart is not a defectiveness inherent in the non-episcopal ordination of the individual ministers of one or more of the churches; it is, rather, the defectiveness of the churches themselves, and, in the case which Limuru is considering, the defectiveness of the non-episcopal churches from which ministers have been drawn into a united church. This defectiveness is really nothing less than disunity itself. The historic ministry expresses the unity of the whole church and its continuity with the church of the past. Non-episcopal churches lack this sign; but it does not necessarily follow that their ministries are not authentic ministries of Christ in his universal church. What needs to be remedied, if the churches are to move into closer unity, is not a defect of ordination which makes it impossible to recognize non-episcopally ordained ministers as other than laymen. It is schism itself which has to be healed; and the ending of schism is signified by the uniting of churches in an organic union of which episcopal order is an outward and visible sign. Those ministers of the united churches who have not been ordained episcopally are now recognized by the bishop as being true ministers of the word and sacraments by virtue of their non-episcopal ordination; they are received into communion with him, act henceforth with his authority, and work with him under his pastoral care and leadership. Since they, with their lay people, are no longer in a state of separation but have been integrated in a single fellowship of which communion with the bishop is the visible bond of union, disunity is no longer a bar to full communion or organic union with other episcopal churches.

On this view it is churches rather than individual ministers which are 'episcopally ordered'. A church is episcopal because it possesses bishops in the historic succession, not because all its clergy, individually, were ordained by bishops. For, as the Limuru report so clearly states, ordination must be seen in a wider context. It is not true that the apostolic succession of bishops and the episcopal ordination of priests maintains the church in being and secures its link with Christ. The ministry does not create the church, so that without it there could be no church; nor does the unity and the catholicity of the church depend exclusively upon its possession of the historic episcopate. The ministry is but one of many aspects of the church's life and worship which mediate to it, and give visible and concrete expression to, the apostolicity and catholicity of its faith and mission. The 'apostolic succession' is, or should be, embodied and manifested by the church as a whole in its service to God and in its witness in the world; it ought not to be predicated of the ordained ministry in isolation from the wider ministry of the believing and baptized community of the whole 'people of God'. All the many ministries which are the varied forms and expressions of the working of God's Spirit in the church are the visible signs of the continuity of the church in the faith and mission of the apostles. The historic forms of the ordained ministry have their special place within this much wider succession; they are not constitutive of this succession by themselves, in the sense that where they are lacking the continuity of the church is broken, for this continuity depends upon far more than an unbroken succession of episcopal ordination. It consists, primarily, in the continuity of faith, of the preaching of the gospel, ministry of the sacraments, witness, mission. Within and transcending the apostolic succession of the church is the continuity of God. The church continues to be recognizably apostolic, and indeed Christian, in so far, and only in so far, as the Spirit of God re-presents in it, and through it to the world, the judging, reconciling, and loving presence of Christ. All those aspects of the church's life which effectually express its apostolicity and catholicity are modes of the working of the Holy Spirit who gives the church continuity, because he is himself unchanging, and unity, because 'there is one Spirit'.

The 'pipeline' theory

The choice that is presented to us by the Limuru statement is nothing new. Basically, it is whether we understand episcopal order in terms of a 'pipeline' transmission of the grace of orders, or whether we interpret it as an expression, within the complex variety of the work of the Spirit in the church's life and ministry, of the unity of Christian people in the historic and continuing apostolic mission to the world. The historic episcopate, on this view, is a sign of the church's commission from its Lord and of the grace which he imparts to it through his Spirit; it is not an indispensable channel of authority and grace to an ordained ministry on which the maintenance of Christ's sacraments depends.

It should scarcely be necessary nowadays to bring forward arguments to show that the theory of the 'pipeline' has been discredited on theological and historical grounds. It is now nearly thirty years since the appearance of K. E. Kirk's *The Apostolic Ministry*,[3] the last major attempt to revive the doctrine of an 'essential ministry', identified exclusively with the historic episcopate, and the Statement on the Doctrine of the Ministry agreed by the Anglican–Roman Catholic International Commission, *Ministry and Ordination*, shows how far the thinking of these churches has moved during that time. This Statement clearly recognizes that the full emergence of the threefold ministry of bishop, presbyter and deacon 'required a longer period than the apostolic age', that the early churches exhibited 'diversity in the structure of pastoral ministry', and that 'the terms "bishop" and "presbyter" could be applied to the same man or to men with identical or very similar functions'.[4] Like the Limuru Report, this Statement asserts that the ordained ministry can only be rightly understood within the broader context of various ministries, all of which are the work of one and the same Spirit. It regards responsibility for oversight (*episcopē*) as 'an essential element in the ordained ministry'; it nowhere suggests that it is essential, in the sense that otherwise there would be no true church, that *episcopē* should be exercised exclusively by bishops in the historic succession. Its positive interpretation of 'what is meant in our two traditions by ordination in the apostolic succession' comprises two main points. First, the ordination of a presbyter by the bishop, with the presbyters who are present joining with him in the laying on of hands, 'signifies the shared nature of the commission entrusted to him'. Secondly, the participation of other bishops in the consecration of a new bishop signifies that the new bishop and his church are within the communion of churches and also, because they are representatives of their churches in fidelity to the teaching and mission of the apostles, it ensures the historical continuity of this church with the apostolic church and of its bishop with the original ministry of the apostles. 'The communion of the churches in mission, faith and holiness, through time and space, is thus symbolized and maintained by the bishop.'[5]

The importance of this interpretation of apostolic succession lies chiefly in the way in which it transfers the concept from the chain of ministerial succession to the wider continuity of the church. Within this continuity the bishop acts as a focus and symbol of the communion of the churches through space and time. This strongly reinforces the view, implicit in the Limuru statement, that, since it is a church, rather than the individual minister, which is 'episcopally ordered', a minister from another church may enter into its episcopally ordered life and ministry by the act of joining it; and the means by which he comes to join it and be integrated into it is by coming to be in communion with the bishop who 'symbolizes and maintains the communion of the churches in mission, faith and holiness, through time and space'.

The evidence of the early church

This concept of the significance of the bishop's office and function is by no means a novelty. It is on these grounds that the historic episcopate is generally valued and defended today, but the roots of this interpretation run deep down to the very beginnings of the historic threefold ministry. Ignatius and his fellow bishops presumably ordained their presbyters and deacons, but Ignatius makes no mention of this function. The bishop is for him the focus and the safeguard of the unity of the church. To be in communion with him, to 'do nothing without the bishop', is to share in the life of the authentic church of Christ. Where the bishop or his deputy presides, there is the church's eucharist. To separate oneself from the congregation that gathers round the bishop is to be in schism. The bishop symbolizes and represents the presence of God the Father, as the deacon, the servant, represents Christ.[6] It is the presbyters, orchestrated around the bishop, who stand for Christ's apostles; for Ignatius' bishop is nowhere said to be a successor of the apostles or to be himself an apostle as having been incorporated into the 'apostolic college' – a modern notion which can claim little support from the Fathers. It is not because he stands in an historic succession, not because he is the exclusively authorized channel through which the grace of priesthood is handed on in ordination, that the bishop's ministry, in Ignatius' view, is so essential to the life of the church. It is because, at a time when the churches are threatened by Judaistic counter-propaganda, docetic heresy, and a tendency among church members to fall away into schisms, the bishop as chief pastor, teacher, and leader in liturgy and administration, stands as the focal point of unity. The cohesion of the local church depends upon him;

he is the outward sign by which the catholic church can be distinguished from heretical and schismatic congregations. Ignatius may, certainly, have attached importance to the regularity of ordination in the churches, but he does not speak about this. He lays the emphasis, rather, on the vital necessity for clergy and laity to be in communion with the bishop.

Here is a very early pointer in the direction of Limuru, and it is reinforced by two important aspects of the early church's thought and practice concerning the ministry. One is the central importance attached to *office*: to the regular appointment of ministers, and especially of bishops to their sees. Ordination of deacons by the bishop and of presbyters by the bishop in conjunction with existing presbyters, and consecration of bishops by the bishops of neighbouring sees became universally established practices during the second century, apart from the peculiar and still obscure case of the bishop of Alexandria. Yet what was most important was the fact that a bishop duly succeeded to a vacant see by the recognized legitimate procedure, rather than the mere fact of his canonical consecration; hence the historic succession of the episcopate was a succession of bishops in their sees rather than merely a succession of consecrations. There is no need to develop this theme which was fully treated as long ago as 1918 in C. H. Turner's celebrated essay in H. B. Swete's *Essays on the Early History of the Church and the Ministry*.[7] It is no long step from the realization of this fact to the recognition that what makes a minister a presbyter of the catholic church is not merely that he has been ordained by a bishop but that he exercises certain functions in the church, holds a particular office within it, and is duly acknowledged by the bishop to be doing so with his approval and under his authority. From this position it is, again, no great step to the further recognition that, provided always that he is acknowledged to be a true minister of the word and sacraments by virtue of his non-episcopal ordination, a minister from another church is now a presbyter of the catholic church because, *without* having been ordained by a bishop, he now performs the functions of a presbyter in communion with the bishop and with his authority.

The other relevant aspect of early Christian thought and practice is the manner in which Augustine, in attempting to heal the Donatist schism, was prepared to justify the incorporation of ex-Donatist presbyters into the ministry of the catholic church. In his doctrine of baptism he had provided a more clearly thought-out and thoroughly articulated rationale for what had been the practice of Rome and the opponents of Cyprian in the third century. This practice was to refrain from baptizing (as Cyprian would express it) or re-baptizing (as it would seem to Stephen of Rome) those who had been baptized by schismatics and subsequently joined the catholic church. According to Augustine the baptism which such people had received was authentic Christian baptism. It must not, therefore, be repeated. Yet until these baptized people enter the catholic church their baptism remains inefficacious. It is like a frozen credit. It is, as it were, in suspense, for it was conferred outside the sphere of the Holy Spirit whose chief mode of operation is charity; schism negates charity, so it can only be when these baptized persons abandon their schism and enter the fellowship where charity reigns that the grace of their baptism is released and can come alive.

Augustine was prepared to apply a similar principle to ordination. Donatist presbyters and bishops were really, or validly, ordained; but the grace of their ordination could not become efficacious until they came over into the true church, the sphere of the Spirit of love and unity. When they did so, it would be possible for them to exercise their existing orders, without reordination, as bishops and presbyters of the catholic church. Again, it is the fact that they are now within the church, in communion with the bishops who symbolize and guarantee its unity in the Spirit, that matters essentially, not the status of their original ordination. On the analogy of Augustine's doctrine of baptism, their ordination could be regarded as authentic because ordination is Christ's sacrament, not the church's. The fact that Donatist bishops and clergy could claim an unbroken succession by consecration and ordination from the hierarchy of the church before the schism began was not really relevant to the question, for the schism had broken the apostolic succession as it was then understood: the succession of bishops duly appointed to vacant sees.

Conclusion

We ourselves would not wish to assert that non-episcopal ministers were ordained outside the sphere of the Holy Spirit of love, nor that their ordination was inefficacious. We should claim that they were ordained by Christ with his ordination. If

Augustine could recognize that by abandoning their schism and coming into communion with the catholic church the Donatist clergy rectified the irregularity of their ordination and could be acknowledged as true bishops and priests, it should be easy for Anglicans to acknowledge as true priests those who have been ordained to the ministry of God's authentic word and sacraments in churches whose faith we share, and who now, by joining a united church and entering into communion with the bishop, have finally removed the barrier of disunity.

10

The Essence of Christianity

In its early days the essence of Christianity was encapsulated in certain basic affirmations about Jesus Christ, such as 'Jesus is Lord'. It is not otherwise today. A modern equivalent is the slogan, so popular a year or two ago, 'Jesus is alive today'.

These statements raise enormously difficult questions, but they do express the central conviction which is the essence of Christianity as a system of belief, that Jesus is the focal point of the continuing encounter between God and man throughout the course of history. Through this human individual the first Christians found themselves confronted by the active presence of God, disclosed in self-sacrificing love, compassion, judgment and acceptance. Through the attraction of his character and way of life they found it possible to share his confident, trusting, hoping response to the providential care, moral demand, and calling of God, a response for which both he and they found the best analogy in the human relationship of a son to a father. In the life of Jesus, and in his death as the climactic expression of his attitude to God and to his fellow-men, they found the decisive revelation of God's dealings with man and men's proper response to God. Through this they experienced liberation from the loveless self-centredness which is sin, and freedom for that communion and harmony with God and their neighbours which the gospels describe as sonship, or as the coming of, or entry into, the kingdom of God.

This can equally be described as possession by God's Spirit, 'possession' meaning not an impersonal, irrational, or one-way relationship, but a mutual communion between personal God and freely responding human persons. As Paul expressed it, believers are 'sons of God in Christ Jesus'. This means that 'God has sent the Spirit of his Son into their hearts', so that they can share that intimacy of communion with God which found expression in Jesus' characteristic prayer to God as 'Abba, Father'. The fruit of 'sonship' or of 'the Spirit' is a character recognizably like that of Jesus: the Christ-like qualities of 'love, joy, peace, patience, kindness, goodness, fidelity, gentleness and self-control'. Where these human perfections abound, the kingdom of God is established, for God's kingdom is 'righteousness' (that is, a right relationship with God, received as his gift), 'peace and joy in the Holy Spirit'.

According to the New Testament portrait of Jesus, his own belief and claim was that he was the agent of God, not only in announcing the advent of the kingdom but in making it in some degree a present and effective reality by attracting people to accept and experience it. Jesus, as remembered in the church's tradition, was and is the effective bringer of God's kingdom to men, the bearer of God's Spirit who communicates the Spirit to them, the Son of God who breaks down the barriers of self-centred alienation and enables them, too, to become God's sons. It is in this that his 'uniqueness' consists, and his 'deity' is discerned in the fact that, because he is the central point of God's liberating and transforming contact with man, the pre-eminent meeting-point of God's grace with man's response, he cannot be interpreted adequately within the human dimension alone and without resort to 'God' language as well as 'man' language. Christians continue now, in Professor Baelz's words, to 'see in Christ the ground for trusting and hoping in God, the example of trusting and hoping in God, and the source of inspiration and power to trust and hope in God'.

This central reference-point for faith in God and love of neighbour is, of course, rooted in the uncertain ground of history. The problem of the relation between the New Testament portrait of Jesus and its original remains acute. There is no need, however, to suppose that the early traditions were baseless, that the synoptists' picture bears no resemblance to the actual man, or even that he was not the sort of person who could be plausibly reinterpreted in the course of time as the Christ of the Fourth Gospel. Indeed, the most remarkable fact about the historical Jesus is demonstrably true: that the earliest Christian documents show that within an astonishingly short time after his death Jesus of Nazareth was being interpreted by Jewish monotheists as well as Gentile converts as a pre-existent divine being, Son of God, not simply in the sense of Psalm 2.7 as God's agent for the establishment of his kingdom but in a sense approaching that of 'God the Son' of later orthodoxy, to whom prayer is addressed and whom believers expect to come from heaven in divine glory (cf. I Thess. 3.11; 1.10).

From the beginning Christians have been trying to find adequate concepts with which to express their central and essential belief in the uniqueness and deity of Jesus as the pre-eminent and decisive agent of their liberation into sonship, into the kingdom of God, into life in the Holy Spirit. Some of these have tended to prove misleading because it has not been sufficiently remembered that certain important qualifications have to be made to the concepts of 'uniqueness' and 'deity' when these are used in christology. Jesus is not unique in the sense that he belongs to a different species from other men. Any interpretation of his person which suggests that his birth inaugurated a new human race, a fresh creation in the literal sense, or a new direction, given by a kind of mutation, to the process of man's evolution, not only makes nonsense of the historical picture of Jesus but (as was demonstrated in ancient times in Irenaeus' concept of the 'recapitulation' of Adam by Christ and in the orthodox reaction to Apollinarianism) undermines the essential Christian belief that in him God is disclosed as acting in and through the truly human; he is the archetype of the authentically and properly human response to God. In the language of Chalcedon, his humanity is consubstantial with ours.

Nor is the uniqueness of Jesus to be understood in the sense that his relationship to God is of a different kind from that of all other men before and after him. Jesus himself was a practising Jew whose outlook and experience were conditioned by the religious tradition in which he stood. Despite his startlingly original and critical attitude to that tradition, he is credibly reported to have seen his own vocation as a fulfilment of the Law and the Prophets and consciously to have placed himself in the prophetic succession. The 'sonship' which he experienced and led others to share was already known to Hosea; the kingdom of God which he made known by his words and actions had already been disclosed to Jeremiah in the form of a new covenant written in the heart. His relation to God is different in its completeness and unbrokenness, demonstrated in the apparent absence from it of the element of penitence, from that of the prophets, but not in kind. His uniqueness certainly does

not mean that, literally, all who came before him were thieves
and robbers.

Nor does it imply a difference in kind between his relationship to God and that of the saints who followed him. They
share his sonship. God's liberating and transforming re-creation
of men is a process by which they are 'conformed' to the image
of his Son, so that he is the 'eldest among many brothers' (Rom.
8.29), and a long and impressive tradition of theology and spirituality, beginning with II Peter 1.4, interprets salvation as deification; men participate in the Spirit of God which indwelt
Jesus so as themselves to become Christ-like and hence Godlike; in this sense it is not improper to call them 'gods'. The
difference between their divinity and that of Jesus is that he is
the archetype of their divinity and it is through him that it is
mediated to them by God. On the cross Jesus was indeed
unique, for he was deserted and alone; after his death the Spirit
of God that inspired and motivated his sonship (never more
perfectly demonstrated, as the centurion saw, than when it
seemed that he was forsaken even by God) passed over to the
'many christs', the 'sons of God in Christ Jesus'.

The early church employed many theological concepts and
images to affirm its belief that the man Jesus was the central
and focal point of the whole history of divine-human encounter.
It seems on balance unlikely that he used any of these himself
to interpret his mission, except perhaps the enigmatic 'Son of
man', which probably implied that he, as an individual, was
nevertheless in some sense a representative figure, embodying
in his own person the faithful people of God who would be
vindicated, and glorified as God's agent for his judgment of the
world, after suffering oppression and persecution. It is unlikely
that he announced himself as Messiah, and most improbable
that he claimed to be divine. The 'titles' of Jesus in the New
Testament, and the symbols of miraculous birth, 'descent from
heaven', and pre-existence are expressions of the early church's
conviction that in him men encountered the active presence of
God.

The messianic title 'Son of God', applied to Israel and to the
Davidic king, signified Jesus' vocation to be God's agent, his
possession of God's Spirit, and the fullness of his response to
God's calling. He was also seen as a prophet, and especially in
the Lucan writings, as '*the* prophet', the prophet like Moses
whose coming was believed to have been foretold in Deut.

18.18. Although later theology used it only sparingly, and with caution, 'prophet' is a valuable key to christology. The Old Testament prophet is a recipient and communicator of God's revelation. He is inspired by God's Spirit, and can be thought of, ideally, as indwelt by the Spirit continuously from birth. Through his human words and actions God effectively declares his judgment and mercy and brings men into saving contact with himself. Jesus differs from the prophets who preceded him because he is *the* prophet. He 'fulfils' the prophets; through this one man, Jesus, God accomplishes fully and perfectly what he had done partially and incompletely through his prophets in the past.

Other titles and images used by the early church have sometimes proved less adequate for christology after their transposition into the very different contexts, first of Platonist theology and then of the modern world of thought. The myth of the virgin birth expressed the conviction that in the human birth of Jesus there was a dramatic intervention of God in history, a new divine creative initiative. Understood literally, however, in the context not of Hebraic and Hellenistic myth, but of modern genetics, it would mean that Jesus was not a human being: not 'like his brethren in all respects except for sin'.

The primitive church could say that God's creative wisdom was embodied in Jesus, and that the word of God which the prophets had heard and communicated was incarnate in his entire personality. It was a different matter when God's word was understood in Philonic terms as the Logos, the hypostatically existent divine intermediary between God and the creation, the eternal mirror reflecting God to his world, the locus of the Platonic ideas, the manifold archetypes of the universe. It was a still more different matter when the term 'Son of God' was not only referred to Jesus in his human relationship of 'messianic' sonship to God but was projected, as it were, on to the eternal and heavenly plane and identified with the hypostatized Logos. Jesus has then to be understood as substantially identical with this pre-existent Son of God, or God the Son, who came down from the divine sphere and became incarnate. No mythology of *kenosis* can then save the central affirmation of Christian faith from distortion; for the personal subject of the human life of Jesus becomes the divine Person of God the Logos, and in the last resort Eutyches was right, from his standpoint, when he refused to acknowledge that the humanity of

Jesus was *homoousios* with ours: he realized that humanity which
is *God's* humanity can scarcely be said to be the same in essence
as a man's humanity.

Pre-existence of Christ as God the Son (or, as Barth actually
put it, of 'the man Jesus' who 'already was even before he was')
entails his difference in kind from all men. Deity, anthropo-
logically conceived as the Son who condescended to become
incarnate, cannot at the same time be said to be truly human,
despite the skill with which Chalcedon united divine and human 'natures', abstract concepts corresponding to no real entities, in a single hypostasis. The classical interpretation of Jesus
as incarnate Logos-Son runs out in the end either into a docetic
Christ or into a dual personality, now human, now divine. The
road towards docetism is marked by the continuing reluctance
of many Christians to recognize the human limitations of Jesus'
knowledge, as was apparent in the dismay excited some months
ago by the assertion, in a public letter against exorcism,[1] that
the church has never required its members to share all the
beliefs of Jesus – surely a statement of the obvious. It is seen,
too, in the similar tendency to understand the sinlessness of
Jesus to mean not that in him sin, that is, estrangement from,
and disobedience to, God, was overcome by his constant response of trust and obedience and openness to divine love, but
that, being divine, he *could* not sin. The other tendency, to
divide his human and divine natures, shows itself when the
miracles of Jesus are seen as the area of his life in which his
deity was pre-eminently displayed, whereas his humanity is
disclosed in his weakness and suffering – a paradoxical reversal
of the truth that it is precisely in his forsakenness on the cross
that his divine character is most conspicuously revealed.

Beyond these christological disadvantages of the Logos-Son
concept there lie the trinitarian problems that are necessarily
raised by this interpretation of Jesus' deity in terms of an eternal
Son, one in substance with the Father yet hypostatically or
'personally' distinct from him. The concept which began with
the metaphorical and poetical quasi-hypostatization of wisdom
and developed through Philo's theology of the creative and
revelatory Logos, the intermediary 'second God', enabled
Christians for a time successfully to give theological articulation
to their assertion that Jesus is God incarnate, and to their sim-
ultaneous denial that God is Jesus, as it were without remainder. Post-Nicene orthodoxy, however, rightly found itself

increasingly compelled to deny any difference whatever between the Father and the Logos-Son, or rather to maintain that
the difference is purely relational. The Son is God subsisting in
the mode of filiation, or begotten, the Spirit is God subsisting
in the mode of procession: distinctions which are both tauto-
logous and lacking in content. There can be no relations where
there are no distinguishable entities to be related and there is
but one and the same being. The concept of substantial relations, despite the skilful use of it in Augustinian and Scholastic
theology, fails to offer a convincing solution to the problem of
positing distinctions between three *hypostases* or *prosopa*, each of
which is absolutely identical, in the sense of being one and the
same, with each of the others and with the whole triad. The
Logos-Son christology escapes from this impasse, in practice,
only by way of an unnecessary and self-defeating tritheism. We
may properly use the traditional trinitarian language in speaking of the creative, redemptive and sanctifying activity of the
one God towards his human creation. In so far, however, as
we refer in this context to distinct modes of his operation, we
must bear in mind that we are talking about the data afforded
by religious experience, that is to say, the different forms in
which men have encountered, and still encounter. God's self-
revelation and self-communication. We are not in fact speaking
of distinct 'persons' in the sense of three divine *hypostases*, nor
are we saying anything about the inner structure of deity itself,
which lies wholly beyond our ken.

Much better possibilities for christology seem to be offered by
the biblical concept of 'Spirit'. In the Old Testament 'Spirit of
the Lord' is one of the many images which depict God's 'outreach' to his creation. To this extent it is parallel to the ideas of
the Lord's 'word', 'arm', 'hand', 'finger', or 'angel'. It conveys,
however, the sense not only that God reaches out, as it were,
from beyond a man's own self, touching and moving him ex-
ternally, but also that God enters into a man's own being,
inspiring and energizing him from within as an immanent,
personal, active presence. The concepts of *pneuma* in classical
Greek thought and of *ruach* in Hebrew are similar in so far as
they indicate immanent, animate and life-giving activity. *Pneuma*, however, tends to retain more of its original physical and
'scientific' connotations; 'the Spirit of the Lord' on the other
hand, despite a very ancient and still regrettably prevalent tendency to identify its operation with supernatural phenomena and

non-rational states of 'possession', comes to be synonymous with God's personal presence. In the Old Testament, excluding the book of Wisdom, 'Spirit' refers for the most part to God's encounter with the spirit of man, whereas in Greek philosophical thought *pneuma* permeates and informs the world of matter.

God's Spirit, being God, is transcendent and free, 'blowing', like the wind, 'where it wills', but it does not enter into men as if it were an alien invader. The inspiration of the Spirit should not be supposed, as it sometimes has been, to involve the suspension or possession, in the sense of a take-over, of men's human faculties. On the contrary, it effects a quickening and an enhancement of their rational judgment, wisdom, courage, artistry, even physical strength; above all their closeness to God, their understanding of his 'word', and their capacity to respond to his grace and love so as to communicate his revelation to others and to serve as agents of his purpose for the world. Even in the Old Testament the possibility was entertained, if only as an ideal, that at least some human beings, kings and prophets, could receive not merely spasmodic and temporary inspiration, but the permanent indwelling of the Spirit as the controlling inner principle of life. For Christians this has become a realized possibility, and the effect of such an indwelling can be far more clearly perceived than it was by the Old Testament thinkers; for the character of the Spirit is now understood by reference to Jesus: the Spirit is Christ-like, Jesus is 'God-the-Spirit-like'.

By 'the Holy Spirit' we should not mean an intermediary divine agent, or even a third 'Person', but God himself considered in respect of his outreach and immanence. As Spirit, God himself moves and informs the spirit of man, not by abrogating or overriding his freedom but by evoking his free response. Furthermore, the 'fruit of the Spirit' is the perfection of the natural man: man created in the image of God. Since man is the reasoning, willing, feeling creature of God, made for communion with his Creator, the indwelling of God is neither unnatural nor supernatural, but the proper privilege of man's nature. It does not involve any loss of human individuality; the Spirit moves and inspires each person in a different way according to his particular psychology, capacities, social relationships. There is no difficulty in the idea that the Spirit may indwell a child (indeed, as the words of Jesus about the child-like attitude required for discipleship may remind us, the chief fruits of the Spirit, love and joy, may be especially strong in children), and that the inward communion of divine Spirit with human spirit may grow and develop from infancy to old age. For a Spirit christology, Luke's description of the growth of Jesus in wisdom as well as stature presents none of the problems which arise when the pre-existent and omniscient Logos is conceived of as the personal subject of human childhood and growth into maturity.

Wherever God's active presence moves and informs the spirit of man by evoking his free co-operation, there is, in some measure, an incarnation of deity, a union of Spirit with spirit, of God with man, despite the barriers set up by the reluctance of the ordinary self-centred man to respond to grace and love. In Jesus alone man's reluctance was fully overcome. In him the indwelling of God was complete, and man's spirit, human personality, was perfected – in and through suffering, since the nature of God the Spirit is love, and in this world God's Spirit in man's spirit must needs suffer because it loves. A christology of inspiration enables us, much more readily than a christology of hypostatic union, to speak of Jesus as 'the God-man' and to predicate of God's Spirit incarnate 'one theandric operation'.

'Christ', however, means more in Christian usage than the historical figure, Jesus of Nazareth, alone. Professor John Knox answers his question 'What is Jesus Christ?' by pointing to three aspects under which there appears 'the reality with which we are concerned'. These are: 'The event or closely knit series of events in and through which God made himself known; the person who was the centre of that event or complex of events; the community which both came into existence with the event and provided the locus of it.'[2] Certainly, Christians have always claimed that Christ was encountered by Abraham and other men of the Old Covenant before the birth of Jesus; we experience Christ, sacramentally and in many other ways, as the present and contemporary Lord, and we echo the language of Paul who spoke of Christians as being 'in Christ', and of Christ, or more often of the Spirit being in them; we speak of the 'cosmic Christ' by whom the world was made and is sustained; we hope for a 'coming' of Christ in glory. In Christ-like individuals and in the Christian community Jesus is in some measure represented; in this sense there are many 'christs', and the single historical figure broadens out, as it were, to include his 'brethren'.

In such contexts as these 'Christ' has taken on the extra

dimensions of pre-existence and corporateness; 'Christ' stands for the object of present worship and eschatological hope. It seems that what we mean when we thus speak of 'Christ' in these ways is not the individual historical figure, Jesus of Nazareth. Though we have him in mind, we are in fact referring to God, revealed and experienced as Spirit, who acted in and through the human spirit or person of Jesus long ago. We recognize, now, God-who-was-in-Jesus, and can make our own response to him, modelled on the pattern of the response once made by the human person of Jesus, because we have encountered him in the writings of the prophets and other 'friends of God' whom he inspired, pre-eminently and normatively in the records of Jesus as these have been interpreted and meditated on in the church's on-going tradition, in our meeting with Christ-like people, and wherever, not necessarily among Christians alone, the fruit of the Spirit is visibly present. Within the Christian community there are many special moments when we become vividly aware of God who was present in Jesus, particularly in the eucharistic participation in God the Spirit, the life-principle of Jesus, the Spirit of sacrificial love, doubly symbolized for us in the images of body and blood and the elements of bread and wine.

If the Christ who is Lord, the Christ who is alive today, is God the Spirit who was in Jesus, continuity between Jesus of Nazareth and the Christ of today is given in the identity of the one God, in the eternal continuity of God's being and his unchangingly gracious, loving and merciful approach to, and indwelling of, successive generations of human beings. It may well be that the first disciples' assurance that God has not forsaken Jesus on the cross, and that God as they now experienced him was indeed the Spirit made known in Jesus, came to them through visions of Jesus alive, perhaps, as Paul indicates in I Cor. 15.8, like the manifestation on the Damascus road. But the continuity between Jesus then and 'Christ' now does not seem to be dependent on a personal, still less on a bodily, resurrection. If the bones of Jesus lie in Palestine – and where else may they be? – this is no hindrance at all to our encounter with, and response to, the saving and quickening presence of God the Spirit who perfectly possessed the spirit of Jesus and is now re-making us after his likeness. If the present state of that human person of Jesus is beyond our speculations, this is part of the general mystery of all the departed.

Our own hope of life beyond death does not depend, as I myself once supposed, upon the resurrection of Jesus. There was already a strong belief in resurrection and in other modes of future life in pre-Christian Judaism. Paul himself argues from this general belief to the particular belief in the resurrection of Jesus, at least in the negative form that if we could not believe that the dead are raised, then to assert that Christ has been raised would be nonsense (I Cor. 15.16). Our hope rests, rather, on the conviction that God the Spirit, who has created our spirits for communion with himself and even now dwells in our spirits, will not dissolve us into nothingness when the body ceases to exist.

Hope looks beyond this, for the individual and the community. It looks towards the 'revelation of the sons of God', the society of human spirits inspired and indwelt by God the Spirit, the incarnation of God in all men after the likeness of Jesus, when Christ can be said to appear in glory because his Spirit is everywhere manifested in his saints: the goal of human history which is not the end, in the sense of a full stop, but is itself an endless progress in assimilation to God the Spirit, from one stage of glory to another, as 'Christ is formed' in all men.

11

Preparation for Death

If the preacher of this sermon is to earn Mere's quarter of a mark,[1] or three shillings and fourpence (which the University translates into 16p, having rounded it down, I reckon, by about two-thirds of a new penny – perhaps one of the minor effects of inflation), he is required 'to spend his matter in exciting the auditory to the diligent and reverent hearing and reading of the scripture', or 'in teaching due obedience of the subjects to their princes and of pupils to their tutors, of servants to their masters', or 'to exhort them to the relieving of the poor', or to 'exhort them to the daily preparation of death (which presumably means preparation *for* death), and not to fear death otherwise than scripture doth allow'. This present auditory seems to stand in less need than most people of excitement to the reading of scripture. That is how many of us spend the greater part of the working day. All of us, certainly, ought to do our best to relieve the poor; we do it in our various ways, and I do not think that any exhortation of mine on that duty would be particularly helpful. Few of us, on the other hand, are in a position to need advice on how to discharge the proper functions of either masters or servants, except in so far as we may all be said to be servants of the community. It is so long since I acted as a college tutor that it would be impertinent and improper for me to offer any teaching about the relation of pupils to their tutors; and I am unenthusiastic about obedience to those who, at the present moment at any rate, administer the government of our princes.

This leaves me with the subject of preparation against the fear of death, something with which we are all unquestionably concerned, since, whether we fear it or not, we shall all encounter death sooner or later and the time is never so very long. Indeed, it seems to be one of the curious features of life that the shorter the time that is left to us, according to our natural expectation of a full life-span, the faster it goes, so that days, months, years, all seem to end before we have scarcely realized that they have begun. At least, that is how it seems to me, though when I talked to someone recently about this pheno- menon he depressed me not a little by saying: 'But mayn't this be parallel to the illusion of sitting in a moving train when in fact it's stationary and there's another train pulling out in the opposite direction? Are you quite sure that, instead of time speeding up, it isn't you slowing down?' Well, of course, that may be so; but in either case the effect is the same, and it is a reminder that the subject of death is always relevant, and for many of us, past middle age, by no means remote. It is a cliché to observe in this context that during the past century the subjects of death and sex have reversed their roles. The Victor- ians luxuriated in death but treated sex as taboo; our society does the opposite. Nevertheless, there was no lack of porno- graphy in Victorian England, and at the present time there is an increasing amount of new writing on the subject of death, medical, sociological, philosophical and religious – so much so that the constant assertion that the contemporary world has created a conspiracy of silence about death looks a little like the continuous clamour of those who call themselves the silent majority.

It is not only with death, however, that we are asked to concern ourselves today, but, more specifically, with 'fearing death', or, rather, with 'not fearing death'. I do not think most of us today do fear death in the way people feared it in Mere's time. Perhaps we do not fear death itself at all. It is possible, however, that others besides myself have found that whenever death becomes an immediate possibility instead of a remote dimly envisaged, terminal point lying far away at the other end of old age – when it suddenly appears as likely, at close quart- ers, in illness or accident or war – one feels not fear, but intense surprise, bewildering astonishment which can be demoralizing. It is the quite absurd feeling that this cannot be true, because, so one imagines, death is something that will happen to oneself, of course, *one day*, but it is only to other people that it actually comes here and now. One may even have the ridiculous notion that one cannot be going to die yet because one's diary is full of important things one is going to do for weeks and months ahead: a sort of crazy reversal of what ought, no doubt, to be a certain feeling of solemnity when we fill up a new diary at the start of the year – a recollection that the future is not our own possession to dispose of as we choose, and that it is well worth bearing in mind St James's warning that we ought to say, 'If the Lord will, we shall live and do this, or that'. Of course, there is another side to the full diary. Gustaf Aulén, who was producing highly fresh and original theology when he was in his late nineties, was said by the writer of a memoir to him to have always been so fully occupied that he simply never had the time to get round to dying. He was a man who made the very most of life, which is the best possible way to prepare for death.

It is, perhaps, against the surprise of being caught unawares by the prospect of death that we ought to be preparing, rather than against the fear of it. We need to be more realistic and less ready to delude ourselves with the notion that our own death and the ordinary routine of our daily existence are somehow incompatible and can never coincide. Yet there is some excuse for us if we fail to bring death into our normal calculations. To our ancestors, to the people of Mere's time, death was one of the most ordinary events in the everyday world. One's chances at birth of living to old age were small indeed. Deaths were always happening, among one's family and one's friends; there could be no pretence about that and no escape from it, and the frequency and inevitability of death and bereavement as present realities, not as something that will only happen one day, when we are old, were linked with a theology which could only make sense of all that wastage and sadness by thinking in terms of the direct action of God; in punishment for sin, in testing faith, or, as the burial service expressed it, in delivering our brethren out of the miseries of this sinful world. I have seen two memorials recording the entire wiping out of large families, one by one, within a few weeks or months, relentlessly, in times of plague in the seventeenth century. One is in Manchester Cathedral, the other at Bishop's Stortford. It was in that kind of world that Mere thought about fearing death, a world which very many of our fellow human beings still inhabit, partly through our own fault, but from which we in the West have been delivered by the progress of medical science and sanitary engineering – progress which, unless we destroy ourselves through political folly, surely makes this, our own, age the best time in all history to have lived in. Today we find it hard to imagine the state of mind of people who were at the same time powerless to prevent death and compelled to accommodate it within their theology as the direct act of God. We may think of Pusey, seeing his wife's death as divine judgment and making his dreadful resolve never to smile except in the company of children. As we now see such things, we realize that what was wanted was a proper drainage system for that house in Tom Quad. Good plumbing and much else on the material level save us from those forms of the fear of death. To a large extent we have been relieved, too, of the fear of dying. Medical science and skill have made the actual process of dying no longer terrible. We may be afraid of conditions which sometimes precede death: the kind of existence which all too many people have to live in geriatric wards. If so it is possible that death seems to us in those circumstances a blessing rather than a terror; we may think of euthanasia. However that may be, we are much less likely nowadays to have any reason to fear the process of dying than to be afraid of being kept physically alive when we have ceased to exist as fully human persons and we ought to be allowed to die.

The whole framework in which we think of the fear of death has changed since the time, in the astonishingly recent past, when to die before old age became unnatural, a result of accidents rather than sickness, and we came to think of death as the natural end of a full and completed life. We have begun to count on being able to grow old. This makes us take a very different view of death. For if one's life is complete, a finished whole, why should one be sad or frustrated at the prospect of death? Why, indeed, should one hope for life beyond death? Life begins and ends in mystery. We do not become conscious of ourselves as living people until we have already reached quite an advanced state of development and become quite sophisticated people. We become aware of ourselves as being here, not as having come here. There are, I believe, people who claim to have some kind of memory of being born, but I take leave to doubt that. At one time, not so long ago, we were not. Many people will say that at another time, not so far ahead, we shall again not be. Of course, if that should be true, those of us who hope and believe otherwise will not be disappointed, for there will be no 'we' to experience disappointment. It is perhaps rather comforting that what Professor Hick calls 'eschatological verification' can only work one way: it can only be positive. Either the hope of life beyond death will turn out to be true or we shall not be there to find it proved false.

If such people are right, we have our exits and our entrances, and what happens while we are on stage is our complete part in the play. Whether we act it well or not, we shall not come on again. We have done our part and made our contribution. If it has been a good contribution, then on this view we have no ground for complaint when it is time to make our exit. Value is not determined by, still less is it synonymous with, duration. I feel a good deal of sympathy with this attitude. We live in, and express ourselves through, our physical bodies, or, perhaps we ought to say, we live as our physical bodies. To depreciate the value of our bodily selves, as has been done in some religious traditions including some forms of Christianity, seems both futile and offensive to the Creator of the body. Yet I have no belief that the value of the body implies its indefinite duration, and the bodily life which is brought to an end by death seems to me to be enough. The body has by then played its part and completed its life-cycle. If there is life beyond death it seems that it must be life in a non-material and non-spatial dimension. Our life as persons, our expression of our personalities, and our relationships with others cannot then, as I see it, continue to be mediated in or as these physical machines which are to such a remarkably large extent devoted to the business of fuelling with food, drink and air, locomotion, and reproduction. A resurrection of the body in the literal sense of *resurrectio carnis* seems undesirable even were it conceivable; a transformation of the flesh into a bodily, yet spiritual and non-material, entity seems a self-contradictory notion which at the same time solves none of those admittedly grave problems of the mind/body relationship which are raised by the concept of bodiless personal existence. If, then, we can be content to find full value and satisfaction in our bodily existence without hoping for its prolongation after the completion of its natural term, might we not similarly be ready to accept death as the end of ourselves as persons?

This is not necessarily an irreligious attitude. It was shared by most of the Old Testament thinkers who combined the deepest devotion to God and trust in his promises for the future of the community with the conviction that 'the dead praise not thee, O Lord, neither all they that go down into silence'. According to Ecclesiasticus the hope of the individual should be to achieve a full and successful and satisfying life, so that his good name and reputation can live on after him and his children and his children's children continue in some sense to represent him by perpetuating his memory. It is not an unattractive idea for anyone whose life has been full and satisfying. I have myself had an extremely happy life, and so far as my own enjoyment goes I should, I think, be ready when my time comes to be content to have had it without wanting more. But this is basically a complacent attitude. The book Ecclesiasticus is speaking for a privileged section of society: people with achievements behind them, writers, poets, musicians, statesmen, 'leaders of the people by their counsel'. They are 'rich men furnished with ability, living peaceably in their habitations'. You can picture them in the ancient equivalents of lovely Georgian country houses and cathedral precincts. The author knows very well that there are others, 'who have no memorial, who are perished as though they had never been'; and he is not interested in them, for to look back on life in a spirit of complacent satisfaction is essentially selfish. What about those who are perished as though they had never been, who might, apparently, as well have never lived? For the many whose lives are oppressed, unfree, handicapped, sad, death must either be feared as the end of any possible hope, or welcomed in sheer total despair, if this life is the whole story. One may say that to encourage the unfortunate to hope for a future life is to promise them pie in the sky, though a chance of pie in the sky may perhaps be better than no pie at all; and when all has been done that ought to be done, and that we ought to be doing, to make life worth while and satisfying for all our neighbours, the fact remains that not even social justice, the provision of health and education, and the levelling of inequality, can eliminate all the personal sadness, frustrations, alienation, and disappointments of life, however much they improve the conditions in which it is lived.

Nor is it really good enough for us happier people to be simply satisfied with life as we've lived it. Is our part in the drama really so perfect? Is there no room for regret and can there be no scope for improvement? What about that curious sense, which I think grows much clearer with the years, that in so many of the most important aspects of life, especially in one's relations with other people, one is always just beginning, just now learning for the first time, just now unlearning mistakes, just being led to see things differently, making a fresh start? Isn't it the case that in spite of all the continuities that one can trace right through from childhood, and in spite of all the obvious ruts that one gets fixed in, one is continually becoming aware that one is a different person now from the person one used to be, and that one can confidently hope to be a different person again in the future from that which one is now: a better person, it is to be hoped, but, better or not, different. Life consists in change. It may be an illusion to think that one can look back on it as a static, completed, performance. We play many parts, one succeeding another, none complete, each adumbrating some fresh development. We are always on · the way, almost growing up. I am not speaking of moral improvement or intellectual developments so much as of the constant incompleteness and rudimentary state of our response to the outreach towards God – which involves our capacity to love and to respond to love in other people, mediating the love of God. All that really matters most in life is always deficient in us. We cannot possibly think that communion with God, that by which we truly live, is ever full, complete and satisfying. That communion is what St Paul was talking about when he spoke of our inward man being renewed day by day. Renewal comes, or at least we experience renewal, in a very rudimentary way, and in fits and starts, however long we live this life. The people who are most conscious of its imperfection are the greatest of the saints. So, at the heart of our life there is unfulfilled hope, a promise and an assurance of the transformation of ourselves into the image of God in which, potentially, we have been created. That transformation cannot be completed in these few years of life; and if those years are all that there is for us, such glimpses of God as we now have are like a springtime without a summer to follow it. Here is real ground for fear, and we need trust and hope as our preparation against it.

Traditional Christianity would associate with death the fear of divine judgment. In so far as God's love touches us and moves us, there is always judgment, for love cannot but show up and condemn our selfishness and hates and greed and our total reversal of what should be the proper order of our priorities. And if the renewal of the inward man into Christlikeness is, as it must be, an infinite progress into the infinity of God, judgment can scarcely be other than infinite. But with infinite judgment there comes infinite forgiveness and infinite re-making. I have never been able to attach much meaning to that strange picture of a day when the books are opened, a balance struck, and the books closed again for ever. Nor can I see why judgment should be feared more after we die than in this present life. It may well be hard and painful, for much in us resists renewal and repels the love of God, but a judgment on selfishness which itself is transformation into love is a healing process, not something to be feared.

One fear seems to me impossible to remove until we come to know the truth about death: the fear of separation from those we love. There is the fear of bereavement for ourselves, and the fear of having as it were to desert those who depend on us. Of course, no one depends as much as we sometimes imagine. But this is a problem about the relation of time to eternity. It raises the question whether we can ever be separated from those with whom we are united (made one). I find it worth while to reflect on the attitude of some religious I have known. By consciously preparing for death and by holding their human friendships within the framework of their acceptance of the reality of death, they seem able in a most astonishing way to overcome separation and reduce it simply to the physical level. Those who have died just happen to be no longer visible.

It seems, then, that to prepare against the fear of death we need to make the most of life: to enjoy life ourselves and to be thankful for it; to do our best to make it possible for other people to enjoy it more; to move through the enjoyment of life into enjoyment of God the source and giver of life, and to begin to experience that renewal of ourselves through his love which gives us the promise of fuller life to come. To make the most of life is to come to be persuaded with St Paul 'that neither death, nor life, nor angels, nor principalities, nor powers, nor things present, nor things to come, nor height, nor depth, nor any other creature, shall be able to separate us from the love of God, which is in Christ Jesus our Lord'.

Bibliography of Published Works

1948

'Some Notes on the Significance of βάπτισμα τοῦ Θεοῦ, βάπτισμα Χριστοῦ, in the Greek Fathers', *JTS* 49, 1948, 58–73
'The Exegesis of some Biblical Texts by Marcellus of Ancyra and Pseudo-Chrysostom's Homily on Ps. 96.1', *JTS* 49, 1948, 169–75

1949

Some Aspects of the New Testament Ministry, the Albrecht Stumpff Memorial Lecture delivered at Queen's College, Birmingham, SPCK 1949

1951

'The Inner Meaning of Word and Sacrament XII (b): Anglican', *Ways of Worship*, ed. P. Edwall, E. Hayman and W. D. Maxwell. Report of a Theological Commission of Faith and Order, SCM Press 1951, 195–203
The Seal of the Spirit, Longmans 1951; 2nd ed. SPCK 1967

1952

'*Baptisma* in the New Testament', *SJT* 5, 1952, 163–74

1953

'Early Patristic Eschatology', *Eschatology* by W. Manson and others, *SJT* Occasional Paper 2, Oliver and Boyd 1953, 17–35
'Typological Exegesis', *Theology* 56, No. 396, London 1953, 201–8

1955

'The Place of Confirmation in the Baptismal Mystery', *JTS*, NS 6, 1955, 110–16
Editor, *The Doctrine of Justification by Faith*, Mowbray 1955
'The Work of the Holy Spirit in History', *LQR* 180, 1955, 196–201

'The Holy Spirit in the Writings of St Luke', *Studies in the Gospels: Essays in memory of R. H. Lightfoot*, ed. D. E. Nineham, Blackwell 1955, 159–200

Editor, *What did Jesus Mean? A Discussion of the Beatitudes* (based on broadcast talks), Mowbray 1955 (with a chapter on the first four Beatitudes, 18–25)

1956

Reconciliation in Christ (The Maurice Lectures in the University of London for 1955), Longmans 1956

'The Lucan Portrait of Christ', *New Testament Studies* 2, Cambridge 1956, 159–75

1957

Essays on Typology (with K. J. Woollcombe), Studies in Biblical Theology 22, SCM Press 1957

Editor, Studies in Ministry and Worship, eighteen volumes, SCM Press 1957–1961

1958

What is Baptism? (Enquirer's Library, 13), Mowbray 1958

'Allegorical Interpretation', *LQR* 183, 1958, 109–16

'Authority in Bible, Church and Reason', *LQR* 183, 1958, 252–6

1960

I Believe, Skeffington 1960

'The Evidence in the New Testament for Early Creeds, Catechisms and Liturgy', *ExpT* 71, 1960, 359–63

1961

Editor, *Patristic Greek Lexicon*, Clarendon Press 1961–68

Discovering the Bible (with D. S. Daniell), University of London Press 1961 (a book resulting from a series of programmes for Children's Hour on the BBC)

Faith of our Fathers (with D. S. Daniell), University of London Press 1961 (four booklets of short plays for children)

1962

An Anglican Approach to Intercommunion and Reunion, Simeon Booklets 3, SPCK 1962

'Ministerial Priesthood', *The Modern Churchman*, NS 5, 1962, 200–11

'Holy Spirit', 'Inspiration', *IDB* 2, 1962, 626–39, 713–18

'Paraclete', *IDB* 3, 1962, 654f.
'Luke', 'Acts', *Peake's Commentary on the Bible*, ed. H. H. Rowley and M. Black, Nelson 1962, 820–43, 882–926
'The Concept of the Mission of the Church in Anglican Tradition', *Studia Theologica* 16, Lund-Aarhus 1962, 155–69

1963

'Nattvardsgemenskap: en anglikansk standpunkt', *Svensk Teologisk Kvartalskrift* 39, Lund 1963, 207–26
'The Bible since the Rise of Critical Study', *The Church's Use of the Bible*, ed. D. E. Nineham, SPCK 1963, 125–44.

1964

'The Revision of the Articles', *The Articles of the Church of England*, ed. H. E. W. Turner, Mowbray 1964, 91–113
'The New Testament Doctrine of *Ktisis*', *SJT* 17, 1964, 449–62

1965

'Die neutestamentliche Lehre von der Ktisis', *Kerygma und Dogma* 11, Göttingen 1965, 21–32
'The Authority of Scripture and Tradition', *Authority and the Church* (Report of a conference between theologians of the Church of England and of the German Evangelical Church), ed. R. R. Williams, SPCK 1965, 3–19
'Miracles in the Acts of the Apostles' and 'Miracles and Early Christian Apologetic', *Miracles*, ed. C. F. D. Moule, Mowbray 1965, 165–78, 203–18
'Hermeneutics and Typology', *LQR* 190, 1965, 17–25
'What does it all add up to?', *The New Testament Gospels*, by C. F. Evans and others, BBC Publications 1965, 51–62

1966

The Resurrection: A Dialogue with D. M. MacKinnon, Mowbray 1966

1967

'Church Discipline and the Epistles to the Corinthians', *Christian History and Interpretation: Studies presented to John Knox*, ed. W. R. Farmer, C. F. D. Moule and R. R. Niebuhr, CUP 1967, 337–61

1968

'The Eucharist in the Thought of the Early Church', *The Eucharist Then and Now*, by R. E. Clements and others, SPCK Theological Collections 9, 1968, 34–58

Introduction to discussion of a paper by Professor P. Jacobs, in *Word and Sacrament*, ed. R. R. Williams, SPCK Theological Collections 10, 1968, 57–61

1969

Editor, *The Cambridge History of the Bible* II: *The West from the Fathers to the Reformation*, CUP 1969
'The Exposition and Exegesis of Scripture to Gregory the Great', *The Cambridge History of the Bible* II, 155–83
St Luke and the Church of Jerusalem, Ethel M. Wood Lecture, University of London, Athlone Press 1969

1970

Editor: *The Phenomenon of Christian Belief*, Mowbray 1970
'The Kingdom of God in the New Testament', *The Interpreter's One-volume Commentary on the Bible*, ed. C. M. Laymon, Abingdon Press, Nashville, 1971, 1176–86

1972

'The Holy Spirit and the Person of Christ', *Christ, Faith and History: Cambridge Essays in Christology*, ed. S. W. Sykes and J. P. Clayton, CUP 1972, III–30

1973

' "Grievous Wolves" (Acts 20.29)', *Christ and Spirit in the New Testament: Studies in honour of C. F. D. Moule*, ed. Barnabas Lindars and S. S. Smalley, CUP 1973, 253–68
'St Peter's Denial', The Manson Memorial Lecture, *Bulletin of the John Rylands Library* 55, Manchester 1973, 346–68
'St Peter's Denial and the Treatment of the Lapsi', *The Heritage of the Early Church: Essays in honour of G. V. Florovsky*, ed. D. Neiman and M. Schatkin, Orientalia Christiana Analecta 195, Rome 1973, 113–33

1974

'The "Limuru Principle" and Church Unity', *The Churchman* 88, 1974, 25–37 (reprinted above, pp. 103–18)

1975

' "Our Father" in the Fathers', *Christian Spirituality: Essays in honour of Gordon Rupp*, ed. Peter Brooks, SCM Press 1975, 9–31

1976

'The Essence of Christianity: A Personal View', *ExpT* 86, 1976, 132–7 (reprinted above, pp. 119–29)

'The Origins of the Creeds' and an Individual Essay, *Christian Believing*, Report of the Doctrine Commission of the Church of England, ed. M. F. Wiles, SPCK 1976, 52–61 and 100–14

1977

God as Spirit, the Bampton Lectures for 1976, Clarendon Press 1977

1978

'Christian Theology in the Patristic Period', *History of Christian Doctrine*, ed. H. Cunliffe Jones, T. & T. Clark 1978, 21–180

'What Future for the Trinity?', a sermon printed in *The Cambridge Review*, 17 November 1978, 38–41 (reprinted above, pp. 30–37)

1980

'Faith and "The Faith" ', *Living the Faith: A Call to the Church*, ed. Kathleen Jones, CUP 1980, 31–43 (reprinted above, pp. 1–13)

'Salvation: Traditions and Reappraisals', *Queens Essays*, ed. J. M. Turner, Birmingham 1980, 63–80 (reprinted above, pp. 14–29)

'Preparation for Death', a sermon printed in *The Epworth Review* 7.3, September 1980, 44–49 (reprinted above, pp. 130–37)

1981 (posthumous)

'Martyrdom and Inspiration', *Suffering and Martyrdom in the New Testament*, ed. W. Horbury and D. McNeil, CUP 1981, 118–35 (reprinted above, pp. 71–88)

'A.D. 70 in Christian Reflection', *Jesus and the Politics of his Day*, ed. E. Bammel and C. F. D. Moule, CUP 1981

'The Two Swords (Luke 22.38)', ibid. (reprinted above, pp. 43–58)

'The Trial of Jesus in the *Acta Pilati*', ibid.

' "The Testimony of Jesus is the Spirit of Prophecy" (Rev. 19.10)', *Bo Reicke Festschrift*, ed. D. A. Brownell and W. Weinrich, Brill, Leiden, 1981 (reprinted above, pp. 59–70)

Notes

1. Faith and 'The Faith'

1. Leonard Hodgson, *Christian Faith and Practice*, Blackwell 1950, 6f.

2. Salvation: Traditions and Reappraisals

1. See e.g. *Church Relations in England* (Report of Conversations between Representatives of the Archbishop of Canterbury and . . . of the Free Churches), SPCK 1950, 26.
2. *Doctrine in the Church of England*, SPCK 1938, 13.
3. Cyril of Alexandria on Heb. 10.4f., PG 74, 985–8.
4. I *Clement* 7.4; *Ep. Barn.* 5.1
5. Ignatius, *Polyc.* 2.3; *Magnes.* 1.2.
6. Irenaeus, *Adv. haer.* III, 23.5; IV, 38.3f.; III, 19.1; V. Proem.; III, 6.1.
7. Plato, *Theaetetus* 176b; *Phaedo* 82ab; *Phaedrus* 248a; *Republic* X, 613a; Plotinus, *Ennead* 1.2.6f.
8. Clement of Alexandria, *Strom.* VII, III, 16; V, XIV, 94.
9. See e.g. H. A. Armstrong, 'Salvation, Plotinian and Christian', *Downside Review* 75, 1957, 126–39.
10. Augustine, *Civ. Dei* XIV, 4.2; *Serm.* 121.1; 259.3.
11. Gregory of Nyssa, *De hominis opificio* 2; 7–8; 12.
12. Maximus Confessor, *Mystagogia* 7; *Ambiguorum liber*, PG 91, 1304D–1313B; cf. 1193C–1196B.

5. The Two Swords (Luke 22.38)

1. S. G. F. Brandon, *Jesus and the Zealots*, Manchester University Press 1967, 340n.
2. Vincent Taylor, *Jesus and his Sacrifice*, Macmillan 1937, 190–94.
3. H. Schürmann, *Jesu Abschiedsrede, Lk 22:21–38* (Neutestamentliche Abhandlungen 20.5), Münster 1957, 116–39.
4. H. Conzelmann, *The Theology of St Luke*, Eng. trs., Faber & Faber 1960, 80–82.
5. Brandon, op. cit., 316.
6. J. Jeremias, *'Pais Theou'*, TDNT 5, 1967, 716.

7. Vincent Taylor, op. cit., 92, quoting E. Klostermann, *Das Lukas-evangelium*, HNT 5, 1929², 214.

8. R. Eisler, Ἰησοῦς βασιλεὺς οὐ βασιλεύσας, II, Heidelberg 1930, 267 (cf. Eng. trs., *The Messiah, Jesus and John the Baptist*, London 1931, 369).

9. Vincent Taylor, op. cit., 193.

10. E. Lohmeyer, *Das Evangelium des Markus*, KEKNT 1.2¹¹, 1951, ad loc.

11. S. G. Hall, 'Swords of Offence', *Studia Evangelica* I, TU 73, 1959, 499–502.

12. M. Rostovtzeff, 'Οὓς δεξιὸν ἀποτέμνειν', ZNW 33, 1934, 196–9; D. Daube, 'Three Notes having to do with Johanan ben Zaccai: III. Slitting the High Priest's Ear', *JTS* 11, 1960, 59–62; Lohmeyer, op. cit., 322f.

13. 'The Enigma of the Swords': W. Western, *ExpT* 50, 1939, 377; S. K. Finlayson, ibid., 563; Western, *ExpT* 52, 1941, 357.

14. H. Helmbold, *Vorsynoptische Evangelien*, Stuttgart 1953, 41.

15. Eisler, op. cit., 266ff., cf. 468 n. 2.

16. Brandon, op. cit., 203.

17. Ibid., 340f.

6. *'The Testimony of Jesus is the Spirit of Prophecy' (Rev. 19.10)*

1. H. C. Hoskier, *The Complete Commentary of Oecumenius on the Apocalypse*, University of Michigan Press, Ann Arbor, 1928, 205.

2. Andrew of Caesarea, *Comm. in Apoc.*, PG 106, 400B.

3. Arethas of Caesarea, *Comm. in Apoc.*, PG 106, 740D.

4. Primasius, PL 68, 910; cf. Bede, PL 93, 189.

5. See esp. O. Michel, 'Zeuge und Zeugnis', *Neues Testament und Geschichte: O. Cullmann zum 70. Geburtstag*, ed. B. Reicke and H. Baltensweiler, Zürich and Tübingen 1972, 15–31; cf. also E. Günther, 'Zeuge und Martyrer', ZNW 47, 1956, 145–61; A. A. Trites, *The New Testament Concept of Witness*, CUP 1977; N. Brox, *Zeuge und Märtyrer*, Studien zum Alten und Neuen Testament 5, Munich 1961.

6. H. B. Swete, *The Apocalypse of St John*, Macmillan 1909³, ad loc.

7. I. T. Beckwith, *The Apocalypse of John*, Macmillan, New York, 1919, reissued Baker Book House, Grand Rapids, 1967, ad loc.

8. M. Kiddle, *The Revelation of St John*, Moffatt New Testament Commentary, Hodder & Stoughton 1940, ad loc.

9. R. H. Preston and A. T. Hanson, *The Revelation of St John the Divine*, Torch Bible Commentaries, SCM Press 1949, ad loc.

10. T. S. Kepler, *The Book of Revelation*, OUP 1957, ad loc.

11. A. M. Farrer, *The Revelation of St John the Divine*, Clarendon Press 1964, ad loc.

12. G. B. Caird, *The Revelation of St John the Divine*, BNTC, 1966, ad loc.

13. L. Morris, *The Revelation of St John*, Tyndale Press 1969, ad loc.

14. H. Kraft, *Die Offenbarung des Johannes*, HNT 16a, 1974, ad loc.

15. Trites, op. cit., 156f.

16. C. H. Turner, 'I Tim. vi. 12, 13: ἐπὶ Ποντίου Πιλάτου', *JTS* 28, 1927, 270–73.

17. J. Jeremias, *Die Briefe an Timotheus und Titus*, Das Neue Testament Deutsch, Göttingen 1937, ad loc.

18. J. N. D. Kelly, *The Pastoral Epistles*, BNTC, 1963, ad loc.

19. H. von Campenhausen, *Die Idee des Martyriums in der alten Kirche*, Göttingen 1964², 50.

20. M. Dibelius, *Die Pastoralbriefe*, HNT 13, 1966⁴, ad loc.

21. Theodoret, ad loc., PG 82, 828.

22. Hegesippus, cited by Eusebius, *Hist. eccl.* II, 23.18.

23. Cf. Justin, I Apol. 4.6; *Epistle of the Churches of Lyons and Vienne*, in Eusebius, *Hist. eccl.* V, chs. 1–2 (here 1.12).

24. Justin, I *Apol.* 4.6; cf. Origen, *Comm. on John* VI, 54: τῆς ὁμολογίας τῆς μέχρι θανάτου.

25. Eusebius, *Hist. eccl.* V, 2.3.

26. G. Baldensperger, 'Il a rendu témoinage devant Ponce Pilate', *RHPR* 2, 1922, 1–25, 95–117.

27. H. Windisch, 'Zur Christologie der Pastoralbriefe', *ZNW* 34, 1935, 219.

28. Eusebius, *Hist. eccl.* V, 2.3.

29. R. H. Charles, *The Revelation of St John*, ICC, 1920, ad loc.

30. E. Lohmeyer, *Die Offenbarung des Johannes*, HNT 16, 1953², ad loc.

31. T. F. Glasson, *The Revelation of John*, CUP 1963, ad loc.

32. H. M. Féret, *L'Apocalypse de Saint Jean*, Paris 1946, ad loc.

33. II Thess 1.10; I Cor. 1.6; 2.1 (if μυστήριον is not read here).

34. At Acts 22.20 μάρτυς may conceivably already have the meaning of 'martyr'.

35. H. B. Swete, *Theodori Episcopi Mopsuesteni in Epistolas B. Pauli Commentarii*, CUP 1882, II, 182f.

36. E. Käsemann, 'Das Formular einer neutestmentlichen Ordinationsparänese', *Neutestamentliche Studien für R. Bultmann*, ed. W. Eltester, BZNW 21, 1954, 261–8.

37. Eusebius, *Hist. eccl.* V, 3.3.

38. Cyprian, *Ep.* 81 (CSEL 3.842).

39. *Mart. Perpet.* 15; *Mart. Carpi* 3.6; cf. Tertullian, *Pudic.* 22.

40. As is suggested by the parallels drawn in the account of Stephen's death and, more extensively, in the *Martyrdom of Polycarp*.

7. *Martyrdom and Inspiration*

1. *Mart. Polyc.* 8.2; 9.2f.; cf. Pliny, *Epp.* X, 96.3f.

2. Ignatius, *Ephes.* 3.1; *Rom.* 4.2f.; 5.3; 6.3.

3. Eusebius, *Hist. eccl.* V, 1.23, 42, 41.

4. Clement of Alexandria, Strom. IV, VIII, 56.2.

5. Tertullian, *Apol.* 50; *Ad nat.* 1.18.

6. Clement of Alexandria, *Strom.* IV, IV, 13–18.

7. Eusebius, *Hist. eccl.* V, 1.16, 25, 27, 35.

8. Ibid., V, 1.10.

9. Gregory of Tours, *De gloria martyrum* 49. See D. H. Quentin, 'La liste des martyres de Lyon de l'an 177', *Analecta Bollandiana* 39, 1921, 113–38, here 134f.

10. H. von Campenhausen, 'Das Martyrium des Zacharias', *Historisches Jahrbuch* 77, 1958, 383–6, reprinted in *Aus der Frühzeit des Christentums*, Tübingen 1963, 302–7.

11. See S. H. Blank, 'The Death of Zechariah in Rabbinic Literature', *HUCA* 12–13, 1937–38, 327–46.

12. Sozomen, *Hist. eccl.* IX, 17.

13. C. C. Torrey, *The Lives of the Prophets, Journal of Biblical Literature* Monograph Series, 1, Philadelphia 1946.

14. Chrysostom, *Hom.* 74.2 *in Matt.* (PG 58, 681).

15. Jerome, *Comm. in Matt.* 23.35f.

16. Origen, *Comm. ser. in Matt.* 25, on Matt. 23.29–36.

17. Origen, *Fr.* 457 *in Matt.*; cf. Josephus, *Bell. Jud.* IV, 5.4 (335–44).

18. Epiphanius, *Haer.* 26.12; cf. Josephus, *C. Apion.* 11.7 (79–88); and, for the similar slander directed against Christian worship, Tertullian, *Ad nat.* 1.11.

19. Peter of Alexandria, *Ep. can.* 13 (PG 18, 504).

20. Eusebius, *Hist. eccl.* V, 3.3.

21. Cyprian, *Ep.* 81 (CSEL 3.842).

22. This raises the question of the relation between apostasy in the early church and the tradition of Peter's denial of Jesus. I have discussed this elsewhere, e.g. in 'Church Discipline and the Interpretation of the Epistles to the Corinthians', *Christian History and Interpretation: Studies presented to John Knox*, ed. W. R. Farmer, C. F. D. Moule and R. R. Niebuhr, CUP 1967, 356–8.

23. See ch. 6, n. 35.

24. See ch. 6, nn. 16–20.

25. See ch. 6, n. 33.

8. Women and the Ministry of Priesthood

1. Statement on the Doctrine of the Ministry Agreed by the Anglican–Roman Catholic International Commission, Canterbury, 1973, published as *Ministry and Ordination*, SPCK 1973.

2. R. A. Norris, 'Priesthood and the Maleness of Christ: Trinity and Christology in the Fathers', in *Pro and Con on the Ordination of Women*, circulated for the Anglican-Roman Catholic Consultation.

9. The 'Limuru Principle' and Church Unity

1. Anglican Consultative Council, Report of the Meeting at Limuru, Kenya, in 1971, published as *The Time is Now*, SPCK 1971, 4.

2. Report of the Archbishops' Commission on Intercommunion, *Intercommunion Today*, Church Information Office 1968.

3. K. E. Kirk, ed., *The Apostolic Ministry: Essays on the History and Doctrine of Episcopacy*, Hodder & Stoughton 1946.

4. *Ministry and Ordination*, para. 6.

5. Ibid., para. 16.

6. Ignatius, *Magnesians* 7.1; *Trallians* 3.1.

7. C. H. Turner, 'Apostolic Succession: A. The Original Conception; B. The Problem of Non-Catholic Orders', in H. B. Swete, ed., *Essays on the Early History of the Church and Ministry*, Macmillan 1918, 93–214.

10. *The Essence of Christianity*

1. G. W. H. Lampe and Don Cupitt, 'An Open Letter on Exorcism', reprinted in Don Cupitt, *Explorations in Theology* 6, SCM Press 1979, 50f.

2. John Knox, *On the Meaning of Christ*, reprinted in *Jesus, Lord and Christ*, Harper & Bros. 1958, 205f.

11. *Preparation for Death*

1. John Mere, Registrary of the University of Cambridge, died on 13 April 1558 and was buried in St Benet's Church. He left an endowment for a University Sermon to be preached in that church each year on the first day of the Easter Term. This sermon was preached on Tuesday 15 April 1980.

Index of Authors and Works

Hoskier, H., 144
Hoskyns, E., 14

Ignatius, 64f., 73, 78, 97, 143,
   145, 147
Inge, W. R., 89
Intercommunion Today, 104, 146
Irenaeus, 23f., 26, 64, 87, 121,
   143
Isaiah, book of, 28, 38f., 47–51,
   54–6, 76
Isaiah, Martyrdom of, 77

James, epistle of, 12, 68
James, Protevangelium of, 81
Jeremiah, 121
Jeremias, J., 64, 143, 145
Jerome, 80f., 146
John, gospel of, 32, 35f., 39, 43,
   53, 65, 67, 69, 73, 75, 82, 86f.,
   120
   epistles of, 67f., 86
Josephus, 53, 57, 81, 146
Jubilees, book of, 68
Justin, 26, 64, 145

Käsemann, E., 69, 145
Kelly, J. N. D., 64, 69, 145
Kepler, T. S., 61, 63, 144
Kiddle, M., 61f., 144
Kirk, K. E., 114, 147
Klostermann, E., 47, 144
Knox, J., 127, 146, 147
Kraft, H., 62, 144
Küng, H., 27

Lefebvre, M., 91
Lohmeyer, 52f., 144, 145
Luke, gospel of, 43–58, 60, 63f.,
   67–9, 75, 77–9, 81–4, 87
*Lyons and Vienne, Epistle of the
   Churches of*, 65, 69, 72f., 75,
   78f., 82, 145

Maccabees, books of, 71, 74f., 77
Mark, gospel of, 43f., 46, 51–6,
   63f., 67f., 74, 77, 82–4, 87
Matthew, gospel of, 43–6, 53,

63f., 67–9, 74, 77f., 80–84, 87,
   100
Matthews, W. R., 89
Maximus Confessor, 27, 143
Mere, J., 130f., 147
Michel, O., 144
Ministry and Ordination, 114,
   146f.
Morris, L., 62, 144

Neale, J. M., 107
Norris, R. A., 98, 146

Oecumenius, 59f., 144
Origen, 22, 26, 81, 145, 146

Papias, 26
Paul, Pauline epistles, 7, 12, 18,
   20, 24, 26f., 29, 32, 48, 61, 63,
   66, 68, 73, 77, 85f., 93–5, 119–
   21, 128f., 136f., 145
Perpetua, Martyrdom of, 75, 145
Peter, epistles of, 24, 46, 73, 75,
   78, 86, 121
Peter of Alexandria, 81, 146
Philo, 33f., 92
Plato, Platonism, 33, 143
Pliny, 145
Plotinus, 26, 143
Polycarp, 66, 88
Polycarp, Martyrdom of, 64, 69,
   72f., 75, 87
Preston, R. H., 61, 144
Primasius, 60, 144
Proverbs, book of, 33
Psalms, book of, 24, 39, 52, 65,
   76, 121, 134f.
Pusey, E. B., 133

Quentin, D. H., 146

Raven, C. E., 89
Revelation, book of, 59–70, 75,
   86–8
Rostovtzeff, M., 53, 144

Schürmann, H., 44f., 143
Sozomen, 79f., 146